Sin is serious. But you can f   ⁄ou
why obeying God is better by ɪaɪ ɯɑɴ ɯ....g .

Collin Hansen
Editorial Director, The Gospel Coalition;
Co-author, 'A God-Sized Vision: Revival Stories That Stretch and Stir'

Conventional wisdom in this pragmatic age of ours insists that it's always easier to ask forgiveness than to ask permission. Scripture says almost the exact opposite: "To obey is better than sacrifice" (1 Sam. 15:22). David Hegg has written this very helpful book to show why obedience to God is always the best of all our choices. Carefully, skillfully tracing the theme through several passages of Scripture, he shows why obedience is not merely our duty; it can also be our delight. Easy to read and yet thought provoking, this is a fine book on a supremely important topic.

John MacArthur
Pastor, Grace Community Church, Sun Valley, California

Written by a veteran pastor, this well-informed book encourages and challenges us to think about crucial truths at the intersection of faith and practice.

Michael Horton
J. Gresham Machen Professor of Systematic Theology and Apologetics,
Westminster Seminary in California, Escondido, California

The Obedience Option not only is scholarly, but it is extremely practical as it not only espouses the benefits of obedience, but practically explains how we are able to become more obedient and thus experience all God has for us. But, in the end this is not a self-help book or a behavior modification epistle. The greatest gift David has given us in The Obedience Option is to proclaim the truth that the only way to overcome a passion for sin is with an overwhelming passion for righteousness and to help us develop that passion. David's writings are especially credible to me, because I know David and his passion for righteousness does drive his personal life.

Paul Friesen
Conference Speaker, Author and Founder of 'Home Improvement Ministries'

In *The Obedience Option*, David Hegg not only challenges the reader to obedience, but he motivates me to pursue a life of obedience, and provides me a roadmap explaining how I can grow in obedience from a right motive. David shows me how obedience springs from faith, and further instructs me regarding how to grow my faith so that it becomes an effective shield against the fiery darts of temptation. Many books on sanctification discuss what it is, and why it's important, but this book provides practical advice showing a biblical path to an obedience that is better by far than any other alternative. I commend The Obedience Option for your reading and application.

Terry Catron
Director of Finance, Intuit, Silicon Valley, California

In *The Obedience Option*, David Hegg has given us a very helpful manual on biblical sanctification. The real challenge of holiness amidst this wicked world is here addressed admirably, providing the Christian with solid direction, wise counsel, and encouraging hope.

If you're looking for a clear answer as to why you sin and yet why you should vigorously resist it, this book is for you! Read it with much spiritual profit. You'll be glad you did.

Lance Quinn
Pastor-Teacher, The Bible Church of Little Rock, Little Rock, Arkansas

The Obedience Option:
Because God knows what's good for you

David W. Hegg

CHRISTIAN
FOCUS

David W. Hegg has been in pastoral ministry for 20 years and presently pastors Grace Baptist Church in Santa Clarita, California where he lives with his wife Cherylyn. He holds a D. Min from Westminster Seminary in California and is an adjunct professor at The Master's College. He is the author of *Appointed to Preach* and blogs at www.heggthought.com

Unless otherwise stated, Scripture quotations are taken from the *New American Standard Bible*®, Copyright © 1960, 1962, 1963, 1968, 1971, 1972, 1973, 1975, 1977, 1995 by The Lockman Foundation. Used by permission.

ISBN 978-1-84550-606-3

First published in 2010,
reprinted 2011
by
Christian Focus Publications Ltd,
Geanies House, Fearn, Ross-shire
IV20 1TW, Scotland
www.christianfocus.com

A CIP catalogue record for this book is available
from the British Library.

Cover design by moose77.com

Printed in the USA

Contents

To Cherylyn,
my friend, wife, partner,
and the best person I have ever known.
Your winsome holiness continues to show me
that obedience to God really is our best option, and
better by far.

Acknowledgments

A BOOK like this is the result of life-on-life experiences among those running the race of faith together. Over many years I have been privileged to run with great men and women for whom the pursuit of righteousness has become a delight.

My thanks to the servant-warriors of Pacific Lutheran University Football who first stirred in me the need to address this topic. Thanks to Frosty and Donna Westering, Scott and Susan Westering, Phil and Krista Olafson, Paul and Julie Finley, Craig and Karen Kupp, Chris and Jen Havel, Frank and Tracie Johnson and all the rest who first heard about the obedience option. *Go Lutes!*

Thanks also to the brothers who gathered every Wednesday morning to study God's Word over my years at Northpoint Evangelical Free Church. You truly are 'men of the Word', and without you this book would never have been born. I will always treasure our time together.

Thank you as well to the Grace family for letting me minister in my sweet spots, for delighting in the preaching of God's Word, and for diligently pursuing the obedience option as a congregation. God's ways truly are better by far, and I am so excited to pursue them together. We are the people of God, and it is our daily privilege to go out and live like it!

My appreciation also goes out to Linda Shada, whose careful handling of my schedule allowed time to complete this project, and to Martha Harding who provided much needed proofreading assistance.

Lastly, to my wife Cherylyn I owe a lifetime of thanks. Your enduring confidence in me, your encouraging love for me, and your lifelong partnership with me have made our family and ministry adventures pure joy. Thanks Bert!

Greatness in the kingdom of God is measured in terms of obedience.

JOHN STOTT

Introduction

I'VE never been quite sure just what an 'Introduction' is supposed to do for a book, or for you the reader. But since you and I have at least one thing in common – we actually read introductions! – I will try to make this one beneficial.

I want you to know why and how I have come to write this book. You and I both know that Solomon was right when he warned his son that the writing of books is endless (Eccles. 12:12). And we both know why books keep getting written: We humans just never get it so right that the discussion ends. There is always a new idea, even on old subjects, and there are always readers searching for the newest and best information. Unfortunately, this book is neither a new idea nor an offering of the latest innovation in spiritual living. In fact, everything written here has been said before by guys more qualified to say it. So, if you're looking for the next big formula to follow in order to achieve spiritual success, you won't find it here.

Frankly, the fact that so many are looking for a formula or recipe that promises spiritual wealth is part of the reason that I have written this book. The quest for immediate gratification that is so prevalent in our society has overtaken the religious world as well. We want righteousness, and we want it right now, in large doses, at little or no cost. What we want is spiritual nourishment and health the way Rachael Ray offers food on her *30 Minute Meals.* Now, don't get me wrong. I actually watch Ms Ray and think she does a great job making food simple and affordable. I just don't think her method is transferable to the challenge we all face of living righteously before a holy God in the middle of a broken world. We can't settle for a simple recipe; we need a sustainable strategy.

For years in my youth I lived for athletic competition. Back in those days before club soccer and travel teams, we played every sport and I filled my life with football, basketball, and baseball, throwing in a bit of golf with my buddies in the summer. Like most athletes, I developed a personal strategy in each sport that included everything from developing and maintaining focus in practice to making those split-second game decisions. Physical fitness was also a big part of the programme, as was mental preparation for each contest. In short, it was a lot of work! But looking back at those years, I have concluded two things.

First, while I probably won more than I lost, it was always about more than the game. I came to love the entire regimen that was competition – the practices, the preparation and the games. I loved everything about it, even though it was hard work, was often painful, and as in the case of losing a championship game, quite devastating.

The second thing I learned is that there was no formula for winning, no recipe that I could follow to guarantee success, simply because every contest involved variables I could not control. As an athlete, I learned to pour all my energies into being prepared physically and mentally to make the best decisions and complete every athletic task in a way that put me in a position to be successful. The only thing I had any control over was myself.

After my athletic days ended, I found myself involved in the lives of college athletes, leading Bible studies on the campus of Pacific Lutheran University (home to one of the winningest programmes in the history of small college football: *Go Lutes!*).

On Thursdays I used to find a spot on campus and meet with ten to fifteen football players for fifteen minutes each as a kind of spiritual check-up. Back in those days, we were still using the 'formula' type of discipleship training. In fact, I had put together a basic formula or 'recipe' for spiritual growth, and these little meetings were intended to hold guys 'accountable' (remember that word?) for doing the things on the discipleship task list. It was there with those men that I first began to understand that you could keep all the rules, check off all the boxes, and fail miserably in the business of righteous living.

All too often I would hear guys tell me, 'David, I really had a great week! I read all the chapters, and prayed every day, and even did the memory verse. But … one thing, uh, didn't go so well. I kind of messed up with my girlfriend on Saturday night after we beat Linfield, and uh, well … you know … we had sex.' I can still remember the cold block of concrete that would hit my stomach at those times, and the thought that barged into my mind: 'I don't know what to say to that. How can a guy who wants to be righteous, and reads his Bible, and prays, and even "hides God's Word in his heart" still get run over by temptations? How come a guy who follows the "recipe" ends up with a rotten taste in his soul?'

In the twenty-plus years since then, those questions have pushed their way into my personal and professional life time after time. And every time they drove me back to the Bible for answers. Along the way, I've had to evaluate almost everything I've ever believed about the nature of the human heart, the mechanics of sin, and the crucial part faith plays in the pursuit of godly living. Also I've had to come to grips with the dramatic fact that when God rescues a sinner and grants him or her the grace of forgiveness and begins living His life in them, He does so for a reason. He saves us, not just so we can feel good or have the life we've always wanted. It turns out God is quite clear about that! Through the apostle Paul, God tells us that 'He chose us in [Christ] … that we would be holy and blameless before Him' (Eph. 1:4). The truth is that God saves us to have the life He has always wanted for us. The fact that Paul spends the rest of the letter to the Ephesians explaining the why, what and how of holy living shows that God expects this 'holy and blameless' life in the here and now, and not just when this life ends and we are glorified in heaven.

This book is all about developing a life-long strategy by which righteous living becomes our delight, God's purposes are achieved in our lives, and God's rescue mission in Christ is extended through our loving service and witness to His world. It turns out to be a package deal. God saves us to use us as examples of His transforming grace, so it matters that our lives live up to His holy standards. Through our obedience to Him, we demonstrate the authenticity of His work in us.

There are also some other things I want you to know before you start reading the rest of the book.

1. First, you should know that I am trying to write as though you and I are having some one-on-one time. The subject matter here is very personal, and the tone of the book will reflect that. I'll do my best to anticipate some of your objections and questions, and answer them along the way. It's not quite a dialogue, but hopefully it won't seem like a lecture!

2. Second, I'm going to use the Bible quite a bit, and that will bring into question my perspective on God's Word, so here are my basic beliefs about Scripture. It is God's Word, I believe, in that it finds as its creative source the very breath of God. Of course, when I say 'breath' I am using the illustration Paul used in 2 Timothy 3:16 when he said, 'All Scripture is God-breathed' (NIV). Since God is spirit and doesn't have vocal chords over which breath passes to make sounds, Paul is simply saying that the very words of Scripture find their origin in the mind of God. These words were given to the human writers of the Bible who wrote them down under the supervision of the Holy

Spirit (2 Pet. 1:20, 21) so that, even though the human authors used their own vocabulary and writing style, what they ended up with was 'one for one' with what God breathed out. This is what theologians mean when they say the Bible is 'inspired'. It is from God and has been written under His supervision.

Further, I believe that the God who gave us the Bible has preserved it, through the ages since it was written down, to our present day. I know that there are many today who argue long and loud that the Bible is full of errors. They assert that mistakes have been made in copying to the extent that we have no way of knowing what was originally written. But what they don't mention are the efforts of scholars labouring in the field of textual criticism who have given their lives to the study of comparing ancient texts of the Bible in order to carefully and scientifically re-construct the original word groups. When the evidence is honestly evaluated, it is a fact that we have in our possession what God breathed out.

3. Third, I must deal with the question of the 'knowability' of truth. For some today, it really doesn't matter if we have the original words of God or not. They have bought into the post-modern myth that since we can't know anything perfectly, we really can't know anything with certainty. They argue that since, for example, we can't know what Paul was thinking or feeling when he wrote Ephesians, we can't really know what he meant by what he wrote. At best we can only dialogue on what Paul may have meant until we come up with a 'truth' that best suits our needs. Thinking along these lines leads to the conclusion that truth can't be poured into propositions and passed along; rather, it is always relative, and open to the manipulations of those in every age who shape and guard the culture.

While this belief about belief is ultimately self-defeating (you can't say 'truth is relative' without stating a proposition you assert to be true!), it does reflect a certain ethos that swirls all around us, and must not be simply swept away. While this post-modern way of understanding truth is philosophically bankrupt, those who gravitate toward it do so because the modern understanding of truth as definitive dogma has let them down. The promises made to us by the social institutions of medicine, science, education, and politics simply haven't turned out to be true. We have more disease despite having more pills; we have more hurried and complex lives despite the invention of all the modern gadgets. Furthermore education and political ideology certainly have not done away with poverty, racism, and war. Scepticism regarding the propositional assertions of these institutions appears to be warranted. Even more tragic is the fact that the institutional church got caught up in the modern way of systematizing truth and gave us assertions, 'steps' and formulas that dictated how we should live – these, as well, have often been found to be empty and ultimately unworkable. Again, the growing cynicism toward organized religion, while perhaps a case of throwing the baby out with the bath water, is nevertheless quite understandable.

In response I offer this perspective. The truth of God is not the arrogant dogmatism of modernity; nor can it be turned into the scepticism of post-modernity. Rather, it is the settled truth of the eternal One and has been revealed to us in His Word, the Bible. Further, since He is eternal, His Word is eternally relevant, and speaks to our day, our world and our lives as powerfully today as the day it was first given. Our task is to understand it as He gave it. In this book, my use of Scripture is grounded on my understanding that the beginning place of meaning in any written literature – including the Bible - is this question: What did the original author intend for the original readers to understand from the words that he used? Using the tools of scholarship and history, we can answer this question in ways that are faithful to God, and to the rules of interpretation. By so doing, we bring a pre-modern, and eternally relevant, message to bear on the challenges and circumstances of living in our day, be it modern or post-modern. Thankfully, God is not restricted by our eras; He is the same yesterday, today, and forever; and His truth can be relied upon, held onto, and counted on to show us how to live for Him.

Much of the material in the following chapters flows out of my study of Paul's letter to the Ephesians. While there are times when we'll look at other biblical passages to support and explain the ideas being presented, for the most part we'll be settling down in Ephesus. Paul's audience there was a good cross-section of the people of his day. Drawn from both the Jewish and non-Jewish world, the church in Ephesus was greatly in need of clarity when it came to living in a way that was consistent with the commands of Christ. I remember when I first read Ephesians 4:17 with my eyes open: 'So this I say, and affirm together with the Lord, that you walk no longer just as the Gentiles also walk, in the futility of their mind ...'

It hit me that Paul was challenging the Christ-followers in Ephesus to stop living like those who didn't know Jesus. This meant that many of them were! Much of the letter is directed at the very same issue we are talking about here: How can we shape our lives so that they are a display of Christ consistently and conspicuously? So we're going to Ephesus, and we're going to become local, and listen to Paul as he tells us what God has to say about living for Him.

4. Lastly, my intent in writing this book is to see the mission of Jesus Christ more and more accomplished through the lives of individuals in whom the Spirit of God has made His home. In a world where religious devotion is increasingly being labelled as fanaticism, and branded as a detriment to civilized society, the true work of Christ in the lives of His church has to be more brightly displayed. Simply put, we – the Body of Christ – are the only hope of the world! I don't say this arrogantly. In fact, I say it almost with tears as I look around at a world increasingly plagued by the toxic waste of human sinfulness.

People all around us – around you and me – are wondering if there is any wholeness in this broken world, any joy that can't be dampened by circumstance, any purpose to life given the pervasive sadness that even the prosperous can't escape. They are wondering where God is, asking if He cares, and seeking for sustainable solutions to the recurring challenges of everyday life. It turns out God is actually near, demonstrating His care, and extending His solution. He is shouting to the world, 'Yes, I exist, and I have mounted the greatest rescue effort of all time in my Son Jesus Christ, and if you want to see samples of my work, here they are!' With that, He thrusts us – me, and perhaps you – out into public view so that our lives can be seen as examples of His craftsmanship, and our works can carry the message of His transformational power in Jesus Christ. You see, He has chosen us in Christ for a purpose, and that purpose is that we should live lives that are holy and blameless. Those are high and noble standards, and the work of rescue demands that we take seriously both the calling to holiness, and the delight that such a calling brings to us. That's what this book is about.

CHAPTER 1

Reading backwards

Y OU can ask my family and co-workers and all of them will tell you that I hate surprises. Call me a control freak, but I need to know what's coming. When it comes to reading books, I have developed the habit of starting at the end so I know where the authors are headed. That way I can do a better job of assessing their arguments and their logic along the way. Knowing where they want to end up helps me critique the path they are travelling to get there.

In this chapter, therefore, I am going to save you the trouble of trying to figure out my end game by giving you a broad overview of where I'm headed. I realize that this will mean some duplication of material, but just like hearing an old favourite song, I'm hoping that repetition will only increase appreciation. So, here goes.

When we open the Bible and read it, we are immediately hit with the fact that God has created all things for a reason. History is not just random sets of circumstances and situations that, like a great roller-coaster, are taking us for a thrill ride through the ups and downs of time. History is the record of God's great rescue effort to bring all creation back to its original purpose: to declare His glory.

In Genesis we see God – the first worker – bring into being the created world. As the master craftsman, He produced a spectacular world. Into this world He placed Adam and Eve, providing everything they needed for life and happiness. They enjoyed face-to-face fellowship with God Himself, and were ideally suited to one another. But all this changed with the entrance of sin.

When Satan entered the garden, his aim was to attack God. But, being clever, he realized that a frontal attack would not work, so he aimed his attack on God at what turned out to be the most vulnerable element of creation: humanity's pride and selfishness. You know what happened. Adam and Eve chose to satisfy their selfishness rather than obey what they knew God wanted; they chose what seemed best over what God said was best, and all creation paid the price. What God had created to display His glory was now corrupted by the toxin of sin. Like a nasty computer virus, this sin got into the very operating system of creation and began replicating itself over and over until the entire system was filled with its many forms, shapes and sizes. Nothing in creation was protected from this pervasive corruption, especially not the heart, mind, body, and soul of humankind. If we're reading the story for the first time in Genesis 3, we start wondering if God's plan and power have been forever overwhelmed by Satanic opposition. We are plagued by the question: Will God let sin win?

In Genesis 3:15 we get the first instalment of God's answer, when he says to the serpent,

> And I will put enmity
> Between you and the woman,
> And between your seed and her seed;
> He shall bruise you on the head,
> And you shall bruise him on the heel.

Sin will not win, because God promises to send the 'He' through the seed of the woman, and this 'He' is going to be the one through whom curse is going to be changed into blessing. At this point, we're not sure just what that will mean. In fact, the rest of the Old Testament is really a search for this 'He', and along the way we get all kinds of information about Him. We also are introduced to many heroes whose lives, at times, lead us to think that they might, in fact, be the 'He'. But in every case, rather than turning out to be the Saviour, they show how desperately they need a Saviour. And so, while we are excited about Noah, Abraham, Samuel, Elijah, David and all the rest, our desire to find God's rescue agent grows stronger even as the evidence of creation's corruption is multiplying all around us. The situation grows more and more desperate, making the need of salvation more and more acute.

Then we get to the New Testament testimony of John the Baptist. For some four hundred years since Malachi, the world has not had a prophetic voice. Our hearts are wondering if the cyclical failures of God's chosen line – Israel – have eclipsed the promise that they would bring the 'He' into the world. But just as hope seems all but a distant glimmer of light, a voice begins crying in the Judean wilderness, 'You'd better get your hearts and lives ready because the Lord – the Promised 'He' - is on His way!' This voice, belonging to John the Baptist, was privileged not only to announce His coming, but also to dramatically proclaim His presence: 'There He is! Look, there He goes, the Lamb of God who takes away the sin of the world' (see John 1:29). If you and I have been following the story carefully from the beginning, our hearts begin to pound, and we determine to follow this Lamb of God around to see just how God will work through Him to repair and reform what Satan and sin so thoroughly ruined.

So you and I join the crowd and begin following Jesus. We watch as He does things that we're pretty sure only God can do, like feed thousands with a sack lunch, make the huge waves lie still, forgive sins, open blind eyes, and even bring back a guy named Lazarus from the dead. For all this, we see that the religious leaders of His day hate Him because He makes a point of blowing up their perceptions and traditions. The Roman government sees Him as a threat because He keeps declaring that He represents a new kingdom that has come to set the accounts of history right. All this leads to His arrest and His death on a cross.

What happened on that cross lies at the heart of the kingdom message of Jesus Christ. In order to turn curse into blessing, several things had to happen. First, the presence of sin in your life and mine meant that we had broken the law of God. Since Eden the account of God's expectations has been clear: Break my law, suffer judgment! God's justice is not flexible; it must be satisfied. When we sinned, we incurred a debt against God. It was a debt we could neither pay (for the obligation sin brings is eternal) nor escape. But how could God both judge our sin eternally, and rescue us from the penalty of sin? Only God could figure this one out, and fortunately for us, He did. On the cross, Jesus Christ bore the full weight of God's righteous wrath for our sin. The just demands of God's law were fully satisfied, and curse was turned into blessing. The rebel is now reconciled back to God. That's the good news Paul declares and with which Peter concurs:

> He made Him who knew no sin to be sin on our behalf, so that we might become the righteousness of God in Him. ... For Christ also died for sins once for all, the just for the unjust, so that He might bring us to God ... (2 Cor. 5:21; 1 Pet. 3:18)

As the first bite of the forbidden fruit signalled the downfall of creation, so also the cross stands as the great guarantee of new creation. Paul declared as much when he said that to be aligned with Christ was to experience a new creation (2 Cor. 5:17), which Jesus has previously declared to be 'eternal life' (John 3:16) and described as being 'born again' (John 3:1-8). I know what you're thinking. The resurrection only completes the pattern. Three days after His death, Jesus previewed this 'new creation' life when He rolled the stone away and left the tomb. His resurrection was a pre-enactment of what all who follow Christ as new creations will experience spiritually in this life, and fully on the day of His return.

For a little over three years then, reading the Gospels, you and I have watched Jesus walking the paths of our world. We have been both astounded and delighted as He tossed aside the hypocrisy of the Pharisees and powerfully declared that a new kingdom power has burst on the scene. This kingdom is not threatened by the forces of human society, nor is it aligned with temporal priorities. Simply put, it is not of this world, but it is certainly all about rescuing and reforming it, starting with the sin-intoxicated souls of mankind. Jesus, the King, has at last arrived, and He intends to accomplish the plan of redemption first announced in Genesis 3:15. He is the 'He' for which we have been longing, and now it is clear that, because of Jesus Christ, you and I – and all creation – can escape the brokenness of sin and become what the Creator God intended when He brought us into existence. We can, in Christ, participate in a new creation.

John tells us that the agent of the first creation was the Word, through whom all things were made (John 1:1-3). Later in verses 14-16 he declares that this divine agent of creation who took on flesh, and dwelt among His creation, was God the Son, Jesus Christ. Don't miss the significance here! The one through whom all things came into being in the first creation has now come to overcome the effects of sin and bring about a new creation.

And I told you all that to tell you this: God intends that those to whom He has granted 'new creation' life in Jesus Christ should live in a way that shouts His glory consistently and conspicuously. That's what this book is about.

We who have been drawn by grace to new life in Jesus are declared to be God's workmanship (Eph. 2:10: 'we are His workmanship ...'). We are His intentionally designed and carefully-crafted examples of what lives look like when transformed by

His power and love. We are – like Michelangelo's *David* – God's masterpieces and we are to bear the chisel marks of His hands. These marks of authenticity testify that we are not our own, but have been made to fulfil our designer's purposes. Simply put, who we are in Christ Jesus is the most important thing about us, and it must be the driving force behind all we are and do. First and foremost, this will mean living righteously before God and delighting in holiness.

That's what we should do; that's what we should be. The sad truth is that you and I are greatly prone to inconsistency at best, and downright failure at times, when it comes to living a 'new creation' life. If you have followed Christ for any time at all, you know what I'm talking about. We come to the decision points in life, and we look down the path of obedience to God. It looks foggy at best, and probably will mean some discomfort, even perceived pain, even though we've heard it said that obedience is always God's best option for us. Then we look down the path of disobedience (though we never call it that!) and it looks well lit, smooth, and seems lined with delights (though somewhere in the background our conscience is reminding us that last time those delights turned out to be fake!). At that point, we are in the same position as Eve: Obey God? Or eat the yummy fruit? In fact, we're in the same position we were the very first time we decided to trust God's promises about Christ. That 'first faith' was a decision to follow the path of repentance and faith in Christ instead of continuing down the path of autonomy and rebellion against God. Now as believers, we still face these decision points, and when we choose to disobey God, we call that sin.

This is a question that has long plagued followers of Christ: Why do we still sin? Later in the book we'll look at this more deeply, but for now the simple answer is this: As Christ followers, we sin because we choose to sin; we sin because we want to. Before Jesus rescued us, sin was the natural function of our nature, since we were still part of the fallen, pervasively-corrupt operating system of this broken world. But new creation in Christ, while not eradicating our sinful desires, did equip us to delight in God's ways and follow Him in righteousness. Now we are not compelled to sin; rather, we choose to sin.

At this point I want to be very clear. I am not saying that, this side of heaven, we will ever become sinless. The fact is that any moment we are not one hundred percent glorifying to God in all we say or do we are actually falling short of His standard. We will only become sinless when, in heaven, the vestiges of our own depravity will have been done away with and every part of our new existence will be enjoyed quite above even the possibility of sin. That's our hope, but it is not now our exclusive experience. Yet neither are we still in the same bondage that we endured before Christ delivered us. When it comes to the intentional, wilful direction of our lives and its activities as Christ followers, we can overcome temptations to sin through faith and the power of the Spirit. But we often choose to be carried away by temptation rather than conquer it. My hope is that together we can discover a strategy to make this less and less the case. To do so we have to own up to the fact that our sin stems from our choices. We don't have to sin; rather, we choose to.

So if God has crafted us as His workmanship for the purpose of advertising His grace and glory, and if that purpose is thwarted to the extent that we choose sin and unrighteousness, then what do we do? How do we close the gap between what God has created us to do, and what we too often choose to do?

I can still remember the day years ago that I was slowly walking through Paul's letter to the Ephesians. Being a history lover, and especially the history of war and strategic battles, I found Paul's use of Roman armour in chapter 6 quite exciting. But as I read down his list of armour and weapons one stood out: 'the shield of faith'. I had read the list many times, and yet this time, because I was pre-occupied with the topic of sin and temptation, I was particularly accosted by what Paul declared was possible through this amazing shield: 'with which you will be able to extinguish all the flaming arrows of the evil one' (v. 16).

Up until that time, I had always just assumed that dealing with temptation meant feeling its full weight, and then somehow casting it off. I had also believed and taught that temptations would always hit us and that there was really no way to lessen their intensity. While I didn't teach this next part, I was resigned to the belief that no matter how mature in Christ you became, no matter how strong your faith became, you would always give in to temptation at some point. I can even remember thinking that, as temptations mounted, it might just be better to give in early in the process so I could ask forgiveness, and then get on with life free – at least for awhile – from the growing weight of certain temptations. Of course, I also believed that no one else ever suffered under the weight of temptations like I did, and that certainly every other mature Christ-follower had it all together and never even had to concern themselves with these kinds of questions. But the more I studied and taught and listened, I learned that I was wrong all around. Every Christ-follower deals with questions of temptation and obedience every day, and yet Jesus Christ has not left us to struggle and never make progress. In fact, since He fully intends that we shine as His masterpieces, He has granted us the Spirit and Word, by which we can grow what I have come to describe as 'overwhelming' faith – a faith that, like a shield, protects us from the fiery darts of sin's temptations and even extinguishes their fire.

This book is about developing an 'overwhelming' faith. Let me explain what that means. As I described before, during my campus ministry days the presence of sexual activity between un-married Christ-followers really devastated my carefully-crafted discipleship formula. I would sit and listen as young men cried out to me about the overpowering effect lust had on them. Many, many times I heard them say that, when they were in the gravita-tional grip of lust, they felt absolutely powerless to resist its downward pull. They even admitted that part of the pull was self-generated because, while they knew they were travelling the road of disobedience, the promise of sexual satisfaction, garnished with a cheap view of forgiving grace, kept them from resisting.

One time, when engaged in a conversation with a young man about his spiritual failures in the sexual realm, I really got irritated at him. He started making excuses for his immorality, trying to explain that he had got into a situation where, as much as he didn't believe it was right, sexual activity had been inevitable. In essence, he was telling me that there was nothing he could do about it; it really wasn't his fault, since God had created him with strong sexual needs and urges. When I had heard all the garbage I could take, I interrupted him and asked, 'Suppose that I came into your room and caught you and your girlfriend as you were just starting this 'inevitable' process. Suppose I took out ten one-hundred-dollar bills, and told you that they were yours if you told her to leave. What would you do?'

Now, I know what you're thinking. It is pretty stupid theology to think that you can pay people to stop sinning; that you can purchase righteousness for others if you have enough cash. But I learned something vital that day when this young man responded immediately, 'She'd be gone! I need the cash!'

I looked at him carefully, and after a long pause asked, 'So, what happened to the irresistible force of lust? What happened to, 'There was no way I could stop the inevitable?' What we both realized at that point was a very simple truth: one passion may seem irresistible until a greater passion comes along. The grip of lust was broken by his greater desire for cash. If we take this principle into the arena of righteous living, it comes out like this: the only way to overcome a passion for sin is with an overwhelming passion for righteousness. This overwhelming passion for righteousness is actually a mindset that the Bible calls faith. Here is a helpful definition of this kind of overwhelming faith.

Faith is a life-dominating conviction that all God has for me through obedience is better by far than anything Satan can offer me through selfishness and sin.

In the last parts of this book, we'll look at how the Bible teaches us to build this kind of faith. We will see that it doesn't just happen. Like a muscle, faith grows strong through exercise and opposition. We are called upon to pursue with great diligence the strengthening of our faith, building up a passion for righteousness that, like a good lens, allows us to see temptation for what it really is. The lens of righteousness and faith allows us to see beyond the façade of pleasure to rightly identify sin's offerings as death, not life. What sin and Satan blur, faith clarifies. Sin, once revealed in all of its toxicity, loses its power in the face of an overwhelming passion for righteousness, exercised in an overwhelming faith.

This is the faith that shields (Eph. 6:16) and this is the faith that preserves the soul and does not shrink back to destruction (Heb. 10:39); this is the faith that brings great assurance and conviction (Heb. 11:1), that is met with God's approval (Heb. 11:2), and without which pleasing God is impossible (Heb. 11:6). This is also the faith that enables us to run the race before us with endurance (Heb. 12:1, 2) which will mean more and more delighting in righteousness, and less and less succumbing to the weight of temptation. This is the faith that makes obedience a delight, that allows our hearts and minds to truly prize righteousness more highly than the pleasures of sin, and which ultimately, trains and fits our hearts to fully enjoy heaven, where righteousness, holiness and intimate relationship with almighty God will be the dominant elements of an eternal culture.

If that sounds like a faith worth pursuing, a life worth having, and a future worth preparing for, then it is my prayer that God the Spirit may use the material in the following chapters either to begin or to assist the development of an amazing passion for righteousness – an overwhelming type of faith – in your heart.

CHAPTER 2

Our blessed God

O NE day, after preaching to the crowds that were following Him, Jesus hit them with this penetrating question:
'Why do you call Me, "Lord, Lord," and do not do what I say?'
(Luke 6:46). For years Christ-followers have faced the same
question, and tried to formulate answers. Why is there a gap
between our profession that Jesus is the boss of our lives, and
the way we actually live? Certainly there are many reasons,
but first among them must be lack of trust that the one doing
the commanding really knows what is best and has our best
interests in mind. The first question in obeying is always: Do I
really trust the one placing the demands on my life?

> The challenge of joyful obedience will only be met when we begin
> with an understanding that, in every case, what God asks of us is
> always our very best option. This must be true since He is God.

But how can we know that God's commands and directions for
our lives are always right, are always best, are always our very
best option? The answer is simple, if not easy. We must come to

understand the grandeur, majesty and perfection of God. We must come to recognize the exalted position He occupies, the infinite wisdom He possesses, and the unerring way He extends Himself to rescue, repair and reclaim His fallen creation. In order to trust Him in every situation, we must come to know Him as He really is and adore Him for all He is worth. We will never obey Him consistently until we come to trust Him completely, and we will only trust Him completely as we learn to worship Him authentically. All of this depends on our coming to know Him accurately. For that, we have to turn to His autobiography, the Bible.

If you have ever read Ephesians chapter 1 you probably remember that Paul starts off this letter with a sentence that would make any English teacher cringe. Stretching from verse 3 to verse 14, the original Greek sentence actually only has one main clause. Paul puts it simply with the strong statement, 'Blessed be the God and Father of our Lord Jesus Christ ...' He then goes on to explain, using a series of dependent clauses (remember those from junior high?), that there are good reasons to consider God 'blessed'. Take a look.

Blessed be the God and Father of our Lord Jesus Christ, who has blessed us with every spiritual blessing in the heavenly places in Christ, just as He chose us in Him before the foundation of the world, that we would be holy and blameless before Him. In love He predestined us to adoption as sons through Jesus Christ to Himself, according to the kind intention of His will, to the praise of the glory of His grace, which He freely bestowed on us in the Beloved. In Him we have redemption through His blood, the forgiveness of our trespasses, according to the riches of His grace which He lavished on us. In all wisdom and insight He made known to us the mystery of His will, according to His kind intention which He purposed in Him with a view to an administration suitable to the fullness of the times, that is, the summing up of all things in Christ, things in the heavens and things on the earth. In Him also we have obtained an inheritance, having been predestined according to His purpose who works all things after the counsel of His will, to the end that we who were the first to hope in Christ would be to the praise of His glory. In Him, you also, after listening to the message of truth, the gospel of your salvation—having also believed, you were sealed in Him with the Holy Spirit of promise, who is given as a pledge of our inheritance, with a view to the redemption of God's own possession, to the praise of His glory.

That pretty much sums it up. But now let's break it down.

Paul used a form in this sentence that would have been both recognizable and shocking. Raised in strict Judaism, Paul was well-versed in the various prayers that made up the liturgy of that day. First among them was the *Amidah* which you have heard yourself if you've ever attended a Passover celebration or other Jewish service. It goes like this:

> *Baruch ata adonai, eloheinu v'lohei avoteinu, Elohei Abraham, Elohei Yizchak, v'lohei Yaacov* .... Blessed are You Lord our God, and God of our Father, God of Abraham, God of Isaac, and God of Jacob …

Paul starts out with the familiar words, and the familiar rhythm, but then – shockingly – changes direction. He boldly asserts that the almighty God is now best known, not as the God of Abraham, Isaac, and Jacob, but as the God and Father of our Lord Jesus Christ. Paul in no way diminishes all that God revealed Himself to be in the Old Testament. But he boldly asserts that the Ephesians will be best served to see and know and understand God as revealed to them in Jesus Christ, the rescuer of the world. The importance of this starting place in knowing and loving God can't be minimized. The trustworthiness of God – which forms the basis of our obedience to Him and His commands – is going to be best demonstrated, understood, and validated by what He accomplishes for us in Jesus Christ. For initial forgiveness as well as for persevering, consistent, ongoing trust and obedience, Jesus made it clear: 'No one comes to the Father but through Me' (John 14:6).

Paul uses 'bless' three times in verse 3. God is *blessed,* and He has *blessed* us with every spiritual *blessing.* You don't have to be a seminary graduate to understand that when an author uses the same word multiple times, it must be important! That is certainly the case here.

The Greek word translated 'blessed' is *euloghtos* (eulogatos). If it makes you think of 'eulogy' you're on the right track because that is how the word has come into our common English usage today. The *eulogy* is the time in a funeral when we say 'good things' about the person being remembered. Literally, 'eulogy' means 'good word'.

In the New Testament this word is only used eight times, and always in reference to God. It is used as a description of God's very essence in every case.[1] Simply put, God is the only one of whom only good things can be said. In fact, of all those who could be 'eulogized', only God is worthy of the highest and best things that can be said. Going beyond that, if you were able to say all of the good and great things you could think of about God, they still would not measure up to the good and great things that could be said! His goodness and greatness are far above even our greatest attempts to express or even imagine them. Let me put it another way: You and I could never exaggerate God's majesty or His knowledge, His love or any of His divine characteristics. We could never overstate His attributes. Using all of our imagination, and then wrapping it in our finest vocabulary, our declarations about God would still fall way short of the truth about Him in every case. This is what Paul is asserting when he states that God is 'blessed'.

But Paul doesn't just state it and move on. He gives some of the many reasons that we must recognize God as the supremely blessed one.

---

1. See: Mark 14:61; Luke 1:68; Romans 1:25; Romans 9:5; 2 Corinthians 1:3; 11:31; Ephesians 1:3, and 1 Peter 1:3.

1. The blessedness of our God is seen in His perfect plan

> The consistent testimony of the Bible and history is that the plan of God for all of eternity will never be derailed either by the opposition of His enemies, or the disobedience of His people.

If obedience flows out of trust, then it really helps to know that the one calling us to obedience has the perfect plan for all of history, including ours. The Ephesians must have needed to know this as well so Paul puts the perfect plan of God front and centre. The plan of God for human history, as well as for all eternity, is described by Paul in various ways in his letter to the Ephesians. I will list them for you below, but I encourage you to open your own Bible and read each of them in their context.

The Plan of God described as:

a. *His will.* God's predestination of us to adoption as His sons through Jesus Christ was accomplished 'according to the kind intention of His will' (1:5); 'He made known to us the mystery of His will' (1:9). God is here described as being the one who 'works all things after the counsel of His will …' (1:11).

b. *His intention.* God revealed His will to us 'according to His kind intention' (1:9).

c. *His administration.* It might be helpful to understand this along the lines of the way today's journalists refer to a U.S. President's activity during his term in office. They often refer to 'the administration' when summarizing what the President and his staff said or did. In the case of God, His 'administration' is His overarching activity by which He is managing creation, human history, and all eternity. Unlike human 'administrations', God's is never in need of improvement or change since it is divinely crafted to be 'an administration suitable to the fullness of the times' (1:10).

d. *His eternal purpose.* Paul declares that God's work of redemption was brought about 'in accordance with the eternal purpose which He carried out in Christ Jesus our Lord …' (3:11).

Taken together, these verses from Ephesians (to which hundreds of others from the rest of the Bible could be added) are Paul's way of telling the Ephesians and us that human history is not just a random set of circumstances and events. Even though at times it appears that we are born into a seat on the cosmic roller coaster, the fact is that God is working all things after the counsel of His own will, and He is doing it perfectly and right on schedule.

At this point, there are probably some questions in your mind. I can almost see the question marks above your head like in the comics. You're wondering how everything can be going according to plan when evil and tragedy play such a huge part in the world around us. In fact, you may even be wondering how you and I could ever trust a God who seems so unable to keep disease, terrorism, and other tragic events from invading our lives. Let's take a quick look at this so-called 'problem of evil'.

The classic denial of God usually starts with the unfair proposition that either God is mean in that He could prevent evil, but chooses not to do this, or that God is weak in that He wants to prevent evil, but can't. Either way, if you buy into this 'fallacy of the excluded middle', you end up with a God nobody wants. So what's the answer? Well, honestly the 'answer' fills up hundreds of pages in better books than this one, but here's my brief introduction to the answer: God is able to prevent all evil, and chooses not to, but not because He is mean. He has chosen to construct a universe in which evil plays a major part because it is against the backdrop of evil that the glory of salvation in Christ is most brilliantly displayed, and this display of His glory is the reason God created everything in the first place. Now as to the questions of the part humanity's sin plays in the perpetuation of evil, as well as the arguments showing that God was not the author of evil, you'll just have to find a good, theologically-oriented book on the subject.

But while I don't have time to explain fully how God's plan works in and through and even in spite of the evil in our world, I can give an outstanding illustration of just that. In Genesis 26–27 Moses tells the story of Isaac and his two sons, Jacob and Esau. (I'll give you the brief version, but be sure to read the whole thing at some point!)

Isaac, Abraham's son, understood that the promise God made to send the 'He' – the one who would turn the curse into blessing – was going to be carried out through the line of Abraham. When Isaac's sons were born, God told him that it would be the younger brother – Jacob – that would be the one through whom the line of promise would pass. But Isaac had a real connection to Esau, his firstborn. Esau was a hunter, a real man's man, and Isaac valued that. Even though Esau had previously shown a real disdain for the position as keeper of the promised line, Isaac still insisted that Esau be given the blessing as the new head of the family. Isaac knew what God wanted, but determined to do what he wanted.

Somewhere along the line, Isaac's wife Rebecca heard of Isaac's plan to bless Esau before he died, and she decided a little deception was called for. She devised a plan, dressed up Jacob in Esau's clothes, and together they lied and deceived Isaac and gained the blessing for Jacob.

Here's the point: In this story we have four people, all of whom act wickedly in disobedience to God. Isaac disregards God's direction; Esau disdains God's promise; Rebecca intentionally deceives her husband, and Jacob lies multiple times to his father. Four people, all acting according to their own sinful, selfish agendas. And yet, the plan of God proceeds through them and continues on exactly as He planned it, and right on schedule. Now don't think for a minute that this means we can act in any way we want to. If we continued to read the story of Jacob the schemer we would find that he suffered mightily at the hands of another schemer, Laban. He certainly did not get away with his sin. But this story speaks to the point that God has a perfect plan for history, and that this plan will never be de-railed, either by the opposition of His enemies, or by the disobedience of His people.

My intent here is to show that God can be trusted because He does, in fact, have the perfect plan for all of history and eternity. We also have to see that the purpose of His plan is His glory, and that this glory is ultimately going to be seen in and through Jesus Christ. That is what Paul states in Ephesians 1:9-10:

> He made known to us the mystery of His will, according to His kind intention which He purposed in Him with a view to an adminis-tration suitable to the fullness of the times, that is, the summing up of all things in Christ, things in the heavens and things on the earth.

God's perfect plan is all about summing up all things in Christ. At the end of time we will look back and see that everything God has done was for the purpose of making sure that everything 'added up' to Christ. When sin entered into His creation bringing corruption and death, God immediately initiated His great repair mission. This heavenly mission centred on the coming of Jesus Christ, in the flesh, to accomplish all that was needed to guarantee the eventual return of creation to its original purpose. That repair mission is actively being carried on in our day through those whom Christ has rescued, as they display and extend His grace and glory through their lives of holiness.

When we come to understand that God has the perfect plan for our history, as well as all eternity, and that this plan will ultimately bring about the full display of His glory through Jesus Christ, then it only makes sense to fully and joyfully entrust our lives to that plan. When the motives behind our decisions and actions are in line with God's plan to display His glory, we'll find that obedience to Him is our very best option as well as our great delight.

2. The blessedness of our God is seen in His sovereign power

> The fulfilment of every aspect of God's perfect plan is guaranteed by His sovereign power.

Every year our pastoral staff and other ministry leaders spend time putting together ministry plans and budgets to support them. I learned long ago from my sister to 'dream big because dreams are free'. Unfortunately, I have trouble dreaming big for the simple reason that I know deep down that we often don't have the resources, skills, or knowledge to turn the dreams into plans, and the plans into results. Every human plan suffers from the fact that no one can control every variable, predict what the future will bring, or guarantee the results of every action. So we plan – and then we pray! The act of prayer is our admission that, unlike us, God can dream big and plan big because He has absolutely no restraints on His ability to fulfil His perfect plan – perfectly.

Paul takes care to demonstrate this aspect of the 'blessedness' of God in Ephesians as well. Throughout his long sentence in 1:3-14 he asserts God has no trouble accomplishing all that He has planned to do. What He planned before time began is being perfectly carried out through the activity of Jesus Christ. And how is this happening? Paul explains that his goal for the Ephesians is that, in addition to understanding God's plan, they would come to recognize and rest in the sovereign power that brought it to fulfilment:

> I pray that the eyes of your heart may be enlightened, so that you will know what is the hope of His calling, what are the riches of the glory of His inheritance in the saints, and what is the surpassing greatness of His power toward us who believe. These are in accordance with the working of the strength of His might which He brought about in Christ, when He raised Him from the dead and seated Him at His right hand in the heavenly places ...' (Eph. 1:18-20)

In preparing the Ephesians to understand the benefits of obedience to God, Paul first describes both the plan of God, and the sovereign power by which He will accomplish it. As an illustration of this power, he points them back to the resurrection of Christ. Imagine, the power displayed in that climactic event represents just a glimpse of the power that God will direct toward the fulfilment of His redemptive mission in Christ, that is 'the surpassing greatness of His power toward us who believe' (1:19).

In fact, Paul just can't stop talking about the magnitude of God's sovereign power. In Ephesians 3:20 he describes this power in terms of God's ability: 'Now to Him who is able to do far more abundantly beyond all that we ask or think ...'

Finally, Paul summarizes the ability and power of God in describing Him as the one who is 'over all, and through all and in all' (4:6).

Our God not only has a plan, but that plan cannot possibly fail because He can exercise all the power and might necessary to accomplish it, perfectly and right on schedule.

Now, at this point most of us feel some hesitancy. We're not sure how we feel about God being sovereign because that means He can do whatever He wants to do. Somehow, that seems to impinge on our sense of independence and freedom. We're also uneasy about all that power being concentrated in one place since we have grown up hearing about 'checks and balances', and with the words of Lord Acton ringing in our ears. You may not remember Lord Acton,[2] but I'm sure you've heard the one statement that has kept him in the history books: 'Power tends to corrupt, and absolute power corrupts absolutely!'

The truth that God possesses absolute, sovereign power is indisputable from the point of view of the Bible (Daniel 4:34-35; Psalm 115:1-3). But how can we feel good about it? If obedience begins with trust in the one commanding it, what do we do with our innate misgivings about God having sovereign power?

---

2. Sir John Dalberg-Acton (1834–1902), English historian.

It is very difficult for us to conceive of anyone having absolute power and remaining good because we have no human models to consider. Rather, history is full of the tragic stories of human rulers who amass great wealth and power only to use it for their own selfish purposes, often at the expense of the lives and well-being of those around them. Lord Acton's maxim remains in place because history continues to validate it. Yet, when we put God into the picture, things change.

The two misgivings described above really amount to one big concern: Can God be trusted not to use His power in ways that are unjust? Or put another way: Can I rest in the knowledge that God's sovereign power will always be aligned with His infinite goodness and love? Of course, the answer to both questions, and to the misgivings of our hearts, is: Yes, God is infinitely trustworthy. To the extent that His power limits our actions, even our freedoms, it will ultimately be the best for us, even as a wise, loving parent may limit the freedom of the child in order to protect him or her from danger. The fact that God always acts in keeping with all of His attributes means that His power cannot ever be used to do that which His justice, goodness, righteousness, or love could not approve. This brings us to the third reason Paul gives to consider our God to be *blessed*.

3. The blessedness of our God is seen in His pervasive love

> God's plan is never accomplished, nor His power used, apart from His love. This love never ends and never fails; it is never in error, never wrongly motivated or manipulative; it is as consistent, constant and infinite as any of God's other attributes.

Paul sets the amazing and pervasive love of God before the Ephesians as the final reason to honour God as 'blessed'. He describes this love as:

a. *God's kindness:* 'He predestined us to adoption as sons through Jesus Christ to Himself, according to the kind intention of His will …' (1:5). 'He made known to us the mystery of His will, according to His kind intention …' (1:9).

b. *God's abundant grace:* '…His grace which he freely bestowed on us…' (1:6); '…the riches of His grace which He lavished on us' (1:7).

c. *God's mercy:* 'But God, being rich in mercy, because of His great love with which He loved us…' (2:4).

d. *Beyond complete understanding:* '…to know the love of Christ which surpasses knowledge…' (3:19).

e. *The standard of our loving:* '…be imitators of God … and walk in love…' (5:1, 2); 'Husbands, love your wives, as Christ also loved the church …' (5:25).

You get the picture, and so do I. God's love for us, demonstrated most supremely through God the Son, is to be a precious and ever-present reminder that God is for us! His plan is our security, and His sovereign power is our protection, even as His pervasive love is the guarantee that, regardless of what our wayward heart may feel, God can be trusted in every situation. He always does what is best, and He always does what is right. This sovereign, almighty God, who is working all things according to His perfect plan because He is all powerful, never demonstrates that power or fulfils that plan in ways that are inconsistent with His pervasive love.

This is the God Paul proclaims as worthy to be known as 'blessed'. This is the God we can delight to obey knowing that we are safe with Him. I think this may have been in the minds of the guys who wrote the Heidelberg Catechism, because their first question and answer have for many years provided me with a spiritual vacation spot in times of challenge. If you are unfamiliar with the Heidelberg Catechism, you can find it online, but let me give you a taste of its beauty and usefulness. The first question and answer sum up what I've been trying to say:

Q: 1: *What is your only comfort in life and death?*

A: That I am not my own, but belong – body and soul, both in life and in death – to my faithful Saviour Jesus Christ.

Can you identify with that? I hope you can because this book is all about closing the gap between the profession of our lips – that we love and follow Christ – and the practice of our lives. I can tell you right now that there are few things more difficult or frustrating than trying to obey the commands of God without truly, sincerely, and passionately loving Jesus.

You remember that at the beginning of this chapter I said that God now wants to be known supremely as the Father of our Lord Jesus Christ. This means that the only way we can experience the security of God's plan, the protection of His power and the comfort of His love is to obey the call of Jesus when He said: 'If anyone wishes to come after Me, he must deny himself, and take up his cross daily and follow Me' (Luke 9:23). All the benefits and advantages that God holds out to us are only available to us in Jesus Christ. That's what Jesus said, and that's what Paul said to the Ephesians. Look at a few of the things Paul says are available, but only as we are associated with Christ:

- 'blessed … with every spiritual blessing in … Christ' (1:3)

- 'He chose us' (1:4)

- 'predestined us to adoption as sons through Jesus Christ' (1:5)

- 'freely bestowed [grace] on us in the Beloved' (1:6)

- '[in the Beloved One] we have redemption' (1:7)

- 'you were sealed in Him with the Holy Spirit of promise' (1:13)

- '[God] made us alive together with Christ' (2:5)

- '[God] raised us up with Him, and seated us with Him in the heavenly places in Christ Jesus' (2:6)

- '[to] show the surpassing riches of His grace in kindness toward us in Christ Jesus' (2:7)

- '[you] have been brought near by the blood of Christ. … He Himself is our peace …' (2:13, 14)

I could go on, but I think the point is made. While the plan and power of God will determine the course of all history – including yours and mine – the only way you and I can find comfort in God's plan and power is to know His love as it is extended to us in the Lord Jesus Christ.

So, where have we come? I hope you can see that the question of obedience to God starts with a radical belief that what He asks of us is always our very best option. I guess it all boils down to this: Who do we trust the most to know what is best for us? Ourselves, or God?

If you are a Christ follower, you've already answered that question. At some point, you decided that God was right about your sinfulness, and about the future judgment you deserved. You came to see your life as He saw it, and recognized that if you kept living your way, you were in big trouble. Fortunately, your eyes were also opened to see that God was calling you to a different way of living. He was calling you to turn and walk in a different direction, following Jesus Christ and pursuing holiness. At that point you determined that God knew a better way to live, that He saw things perfectly, and that your best option was to trust what He said, and obey His commands. If that's your story, then you've already been travelling down the road behind Jesus, and the rest of this book will only help you to follow Him more closely.

If you are not yet a Christ follower, I hope you'll carefully weigh what you've read, considering closely what the truth is about God. Give some thought, as well, to the position God holds in this world, and the part He will play in your life now, and on the other side of the grave. Keep reading, and some of your questions may be answered even as new ones pop up. Just remember, you can trust God to provide the answers to the biggest questions of life, but you'll only find them in Jesus.

CHAPTER 3

God's workmanship

IF you read the creation story in Genesis 1 and 2, you can't help but notice that at the end of every day God looked at what He had made and declared that it was 'good'. But what made it 'good'? At that point in history, there wasn't any 'bad' yet, so 'good' couldn't have meant that it was better than something else. What made everything 'good' was the simple fact that it was the direct product of God's creative power. Everything from the stars, moon and sun to the plants, animals and humankind itself, was a masterpiece intentionally designed and produced to display the skills and glory of its designer. It was always God's intention that creation would sing His praise, declaring His glory. But when sin came in, the entire operating system of God's creation was corrupted. Now, instead of declaring the glory of the giver of life, all creation was held in the chains of death.

God's response to this tragic turn of events was immediate and decisive. In Genesis 3:15, in direct response to the deception of the serpent, God declared that He would not let sin win. Rather, in the first Gospel promise, God said that one day He

45

would send the 'He' through whom the accounts would be settled, and the wrongs made right. God set in motion a plan to turn the curse of sin and death back to the blessing of life, restoring creation and rescuing the souls of humankind. Jesus – the 'He' of Genesis 3:15 – put it this way: 'Truly, truly, I say to you, he who hears My word, and believes Him who sent Me, has eternal life, and does not come into judgment, but has passed out of death into life' (John 5:24). In the face of Satan's triumph in Eden, God promised final victory.

Since that fateful day in Eden, God has been intentional in His mission to reclaim and reform creation. This mission is seen primarily in the rescue of individuals like you and me. God's great rescue mission is all about taking lives that are broken and transforming them into majestic works of art that declare His glory. It is only fitting that the agent through whom creation came into being – God the Son – would be the Saviour through whom the rescue mission would be accomplished.

This mission of God in Jesus Christ is on Paul's mind as he writes to the Ephesian church. After declaring the blessedness of God, he immediately moves to the grand purpose to which our blessed God has committed Himself:

> Blessed be the God and Father of our Lord Jesus Christ, who has blessed us with every spiritual blessing in the heavenly places in Christ, just as He chose us in Him before the foundation of the world, that we would be holy and blameless before Him. (Eph. 1:3, 4)

It is very important that we notice two things in these verses. First, we see that the blessed God has turned His mind to 'bless us ... in Christ ... [so] that we would be holy and blameless before Him'. This activity of God – whereby He reaches out to rescue a world full of people whose natures have been invaded by the virus of sin – is what we call salvation, or the redemptive work of God.

For Paul, this saving activity deserves to be carefully examined. In Ephesians 1 the apostle describes God's rescue efforts as though we were standing in heaven, looking out from the porticos of God's estate over the landscape of history. We are given heaven's point of view on the whole mission, and we are treated to the noble and lofty activities of God's sovereign predestination and election, accomplished before time even began. We look out with wonder at the decisive accomplishment of redemption, the gracious bestowal of forgiveness on the undeserving, and the eternal guarantee of this salvation found in the sealing presence of the Holy Spirit. From the heavenly point of view, salvation is the spectacular product of God's sovereign and gracious activity by which His redeeming love comes to rescue you and me. It is simply breathtaking!

But when Paul starts writing Ephesians 2, he describes the work of God in salvation from a completely different vantage point. He has traded the porticos of heaven for the muck and mire of earth. Actually, he has us in the graveyard:

> And you were dead in your trespasses and sins, in which you formerly walked according to the course of this world, according to the prince of the power of the air, of the spirit that is now working in the sons of disobedience. Among them we too all formerly lived in the lusts of our flesh, indulging the desires of the flesh and of the mind, and were by nature children of wrath, even as the rest. (Eph. 2:1-3)

In this second description of God's rescue mission, Paul shows that the sovereign work of God in salvation was necessary simply because we – being 'dead in sins' – were both unwilling and unable to contribute anything to the process. Spiritually we were dead; morally we were delighted with all those things that would justly earn us wrath in the end. Unless something changed, we were, by nature, heading for judgment – but God stepped up, and stepped into our world in rescue.

Paul explains that God, motivated by His great love, graciously overwhelmed our sinfulness with His mercy, and both rescued and reformed us, in Christ Jesus:

> But God, being rich in mercy, because of His great love with which He loved us, even when we were dead in our transgressions, made us alive together with Christ (by grace you have been saved), and raised us up with Him, and seated us with Him in the heavenly places in Christ Jesus... (Eph. 2:4-6)

Paul never gets tired of reminding his readers that the God of all creation has turned His power and love toward a broken world for the purpose of putting lives back together. Paul knew what that felt like, and his amazement continually motivated both his worship and obedience.

But, as great as it is to know that God is in the business of deliverance, there is a second very important aspect to this whole programme. Paul states plainly in Ephesians 1:4 that the saving grace of God has a specific purpose: 'that we would be holy and blameless before Him'. This forces us to ask and to answer a very important question, a question that must be answered correctly if we are ever to understand obedience and perseverance in righteousness as a delightful privilege.

Why did God save us?

Here it is: Why did God save us? It's a simple question, and there are really only two answers.

Did God save us for us?

At some level, we could rightly say 'God saved us for us'. After all, He did come to give us life, and to grant us forgiveness. He has come to redeem us from bondage to sin and has adopted us into His family. All of these are certainly positive consequences that we enjoy as a result of His grace. But all too often we take this too far. It doesn't help that we are surrounded with well-intentioned but ultimately error-based teaching that continues to tell us that, frankly, God works for us. He has sent Jesus to us as a Life Consultant, and we keep Him on retainer by granting Him some of our time, adoration and resources. When we need Him, He has to come running and is expected to make us happy, wealthy, successful, and significant. Almost all of what is wrong in the shallow end of the evangelical pool stems from this distorted view of the purpose of salvation.

There is a growing sense among many younger Christ-followers that this 'God saved me for me' brand of Christianity probably isn't true Christ-following at all. I suspect they're right. Jesus' call to 'deny yourself, take up your cross, and follow Me' can't be turned on its head without losing its truth. If we really expect to change the world we can't be seen as saying, 'Jesus, I'm going to indulge myself, but I'm expecting you to take up your bag of miracles, solutions, and answers to my prayers, and follow me.' Most already think of Jesus as a good man with advice that can help now and then. But they don't need a consultant – they need a Saviour.

Or, did God save us for Him?

The biblical answer to the question 'Why did God save us?' is, 'God saves us for Him.' This is what Paul meant when he stated plainly that our blessed God has blessed us in Jesus Christ so 'that we would be holy and blameless before Him' (Eph. 1:3, 4). God's purpose is to return us to the place where we can once again display His glory. He intends for us to be billboards that advertise just how great He is.

Some years ago I ran across a sentence that really summarized the idea that salvation is, from first to last, centred on God. I am not sure who first said this, but I hope a growing number of believers are saying it to themselves everyday: 'We have been saved from God's wrath, by God's grace, for God's glory.'

That really sums it up well. For my purposes in this book, the last phrase will keep us heading in the right direction. God has saved us *primarily* for Him. This idea is more fully spelled out in Ephesians 2:7. After rehearsing once again the amazing activity of God by which He raises up those who were 'dead' in their sins, Paul gives us the reason behind this God-work: 'so that in the ages to come He might show the surpassing riches of His grace in kindness toward us in Christ Jesus' (Eph. 2:7).

Did you notice the first two words – 'so that ...'? That's a purpose clause if ever there was one! After explaining that we've been rescued solely because God wanted to be gracious to us, Paul gives the 'so that'. The purpose for which God has saved us is that He wants to *show off* the riches of His grace through us! This is an essential part of any sustainable strategy of obedience to God. We simply have to understand that God's purposes in saving us have everything to do with demonstrating His glory.

> God did not save us primarily so we could feel good. He saved us specifically so He could look good. And yet, He has so constructed His relationship with us that when He looks good in us, we'll feel great in Him.

Paul brings out this thought most clearly in Ephesians 2:10, and as we look at a strategy for life-long, delightful obedience to Christ, it will be helpful to take a good look at this verse:

> For we are His workmanship, created in Christ Jesus for good works, which God prepared beforehand so that we would walk in them.

Paul shows that there is a vital connection between who we are in Christ Jesus and how we are to live. Notice as well the divine order: *who we are* precedes *how we live*. The fact that we are 'His workmanship' is given as the reason that God expects us to manifest 'good works'. Our position in Christ prescribes our practice before a watching world. So understanding just what being 'God's workmanship' means must be pretty important.

The workmanship of God

Paul uses the word *poihma* (*poiema*, 'workmanship') to describe how God views those who follow Christ in repentance and faith. This word describes the product of a master craftsman's work, a masterpiece! In this case, the 'masterpiece' is the new creation that God has made out of the life of the repentant sinner. Paul emphatically asserts that our salvation has not come about as a result of our 'work' (v. 9), for we are actually His work. Rather than our efforts having an effect on God, or in any way moving Him to grant us the grace of forgiveness, it is His efforts that have completely renovated our nature, transforming that which was corrupt and dying into a living demonstration of the master's craftsmanship.

Years ago, just after the September 11 terrorist bombings, my wife and I took advantage of the extremely low airfares to Europe and joined some friends for two weeks in Italy. After spending the first week in Rome, we headed off by train for Venice. Along the way, we opted to spend a four-hour layover in Florence checking out the leather markets and other Florentine sights. But for me, the first order of business was to find my way to the Academia. I shelled out my eight Euros, and hurriedly walked down several aisles, intentionally bypassing exhibit after exhibit of medieval art and Florentine artifacts. I was on a mission! Finally, I turned a corner and found myself looking down a long, broad hallway. At the end of the hallway, atop a five-foot platform and bathed in perfect museum lighting, stood Michelangelo's *David.* It was spectacular. As I slowly made my way forward, I joined a group of hushed admirers who stood motionless around what is certainly the finest example of marble statuary ever completed. Over the next hour, as I examined *David* from every angle, my amazement grew at the talents, perspective, and perseverance of the artist whose hammer and chisel had extracted such a masterpiece from a block of discarded marble.

As a young artist, Michelangelo had seen a weathered hunk of marble that had been left out in a churchyard for years. He inquired about it only to be told that many artists had examined it and found its grain to be so twisted as to make the stone unworkable. So it had been forgotten and left to be covered by the grasses. But in Michelangelo's hands, that unworkable marble was transformed into a masterpiece.

As I stood and studied the statue of *David*, I never heard the statue brag or in any way declare just how wonderful it was or how thankful it was to Michelangelo for making it the centre of everyone's attention. I did however hear its silent tribute to the sculptor himself. You simply can't look at *David* and not be amazed at Michelangelo! The statue is his masterpiece and its every chisel mark testifies to his brilliance.

Of course, you know where I'm headed here. Like that unworkable piece of marble, you and I were twisted in our natures, incapable of becoming anything of lasting or significant beauty. And none of the world's systems or powers could change that. Like so many, we were left to live out our lives as broken people in a broken world. But God, motivated only by His love and not by anything lovely in us, took us and – using the chisel of His grace – transformed each of us into a masterpiece. What then is the purpose of a masterpiece? Simply to testify to the skill, wisdom, power and glory of the master craftsman.

God's new creation

Paul goes on to add another dynamic to the idea that we are God's workmanship. He states that we are also 'created in Christ Jesus'. The Greek word here is *ktisqentes* (*ktisthentes*, from *ktizo*, *ktizw*: 'created'), and it is used to describe the creative power of which a *poihma* (*poiema*, 'workmanship') is the result. There are only two things that are said in Scripture to be masterpieces which result from the creative power of God: creation, and the Christian. In fact, *poihma* (*poiema*, workmanship) is used only twice in the New Testament. Ephesians 2:10 is one occasion, and Romans 1:20 is the other.

> For since the creation [*ktisew*, from *ktizw*; *ktiseo*, from *ktizo*, 'creation', 'created'] of the world His invisible attributes, His eternal power and divine nature, have been clearly seen, being understood through what has been made ['what has been made' = *tois poihmasin*; plural of *poihma*, *poiema*; 'the made things'] so that they are without excuse. (Rom. 1:20)

The connection is clearly seen that when God exercises His creative power, the result is a masterpiece meant to demonstrate His greatness. What God originally intended to display in all creation, He now intends to display through the lives of 'new creation' Christians.

I sometimes tune in to a show on television called *Antiques Roadshow*. The show gathers together appraisers and invites locals to bring in antiques of all kinds to see just how much they are worth. One of my favourite times in the show is when some rather unassuming person brings in an antique, usually wrapped in an old blanket, or stuffed in a cardboard box. You can tell that they really don't think that what they have is all that valuable, but they're interested in finding out its true worth anyway. But the excitement begins when the appraiser gasps and then gently lifts the object onto the appraisal table.

'Do you have any idea what this is and what's it's worth? This is an original Himmelfarb and Schmidt! I can tell because of that mark there and this grain here and that machining element there. Only Himmelfarb and Schmidt made objects with those distinctive characteristics. I can also tell you that, at auction, this would sell for $34,000!'

Of course, the owner becomes quite amazed and excited and that makes for good television. If you've seen the show, you understand. The authenticity and worth of the object was only known because it carried the distinctive marks of the craftsman who built it.

But there is a part of the show I like even better. That is when the rather smug owner of a great and rare treasure comes in positively certain that his object will be the hit of the show. With great care he unlocks the wooden case protecting it and carefully lifts it to the appraiser's table, setting it just right to catch the light. He is bursting with pride. Then the appraiser says, 'Well, what do we have here? This really is a most impressive copy of an exquisite piece originally made by Gunther and Glob. Of course, there were thousands of these inferior copies made, and they are easily distinguished from the real thing by the presence of these small divots, and narrow machine marks. I do hope you didn't pay more than $5 for this!'

Those of us watching can tell from the distress on the owner's face that he did, indeed, pay much, much more. He leaves knowing that, once again, the authenticity of a masterpiece depends on the presence of the marks and distinctive craftsmanship of the master.

Make no mistake. As Christ-followers we are masterpieces, newly created by the Master. Ezekiel's promise that one day God would give new hearts (see Ezek. 18:31; 36:26) has been fulfilled in us! And it is this new heart that beats out a new life, complete with a new mind and new desires. We often call this regeneration. Once dead in sins, we now have been made alive in Christ, fitted with new spiritual DNA, and fashioned into an example of what God's transforming grace and power can do. And best of all, it is this new life in Christ, with its new preference for holiness, that now forms desires in keeping with that life. And even though these desires for obedience and holiness may not seem to be the strongest pull on our wills, they are there nevertheless. Our task is to grow more and more aware that following these new desires are our very best option.

When Paul describes Christ-followers as God's workmanship, he also tells us just what the marks of authenticity are. In Ephesians 1:4 he describes the internal mark as *holiness*, and the corresponding external manifestation as *blamelessness*. This is further described in Ephesians 2:10, where 'good works' might be seen as the chisel marks that show the authenticity of a believer's gracious standing in the family of God.

Peter agrees with this when he reminds his readers that holiness is the dominant family trait in God's family:

> As obedient children, do not be conformed to the former lusts which were yours in your ignorance, but like the Holy One who called you, be holy yourselves also in all your behavior; because it is written, 'YOU SHALL BE HOLY, FOR I AM HOLY.' (2 Pet. 1:14-16).

So,

- if God is the great master craftsman and He rescues and reforms the broken and sinful, turning them into masterpieces of His grace, and

- if God does so in order for them to become ever-increasing displays of His glory, and

- if God has structured His relationship with those He has rescued such that they are going to be most fulfilled and satisfied when His glory is most displayed in and through them,

- then it only makes sense that those who have come to experience 'new-creation' life in Jesus Christ would make it their life's ambition to obey Him in all things, prizing holiness, increasingly displaying Christian virtue and character, delighting in good works, and steadfastly standing against every temptation to do otherwise. Even more, they would pursue that noble ambition with every bit of their energy, for the glory of God.

Wow, I think that's a great paragraph. I get all fired up just reading it. And I know you agree with me that it describes how our lives as followers of Christ *ought* to be. But you and I also know that it is much easier to write and to read than to do. Why is it that, given all that God has done in and for us, we still fall short of even our own expectations when it comes to living out the reality of our salvation? Why aren't our lives more covered with the distinctive marks of God's craftsmanship? And while we're asking authentic questions, let's give voice to one of the biggest: Why do those to whom new life in Christ has been given still sin?

The question of sin in the life of the Christ-follower is the challenge we take up in the next chapter.

CHAPTER 4

Understanding sin

SO if God is sovereign, and He has crafted my life into a masterpiece, then why do I still sin? As a Christ-follower, I am sure this question has plagued you many, many times. And since this whole book is about *not sinning*, it only makes sense that we look carefully at what sin is and how it comes to play such a role in our lives even though we preach, pray, and sing against it.

A few years ago as I was preaching my way through Paul's letter to the Ephesians, I stumbled across Paul's request to them. And I do mean stumbled! When I read it, it knocked me into a theological summersault. After having explained the magnificence of God's sovereign plan in chapter 1, which rescued the Ephesians from their bondage to sin, and made them into God's masterpieces in chapter 2, Paul requests that they stop living like those who don't know God! Here's how Paul put it:

So this I say, and affirm together with the Lord, that you walk no longer just as the Gentiles also walk, in the futility of their mind, being darkened in their understanding, excluded from the life of God because of the ignorance that is in them, because of the hardness of their heart; and they, having become callous, have given themselves over to sensuality for the practice of every kind of impurity with greediness. (Eph. 4:17-19)

Does that shock you? Do you find it strange that the Christ-followers in Ephesus had to be asked not to live like those whose spiritual sight was 'darkened', who had no connection with the life of God because of their spiritual ignorance, and whose hearts were hard toward God? Does it hit you sideways to recognize that Christ-followers can become so captivated by sinful practices that they are no longer distinguishable from those who don't love Jesus?

Before you get to thinking that a Christ-follower in such a position is at no risk, remember that our Heavenly Father – like any good earthly father worth his salt – will not allow His children to run the family name through the mud of wickedness indefinitely. In Hebrews we're warned that the Lord disciplines His own so that they can 'share His holiness' (Heb. 12:10). It could be said that Paul is lovingly calling the Ephesian believers back to a life of holiness so that they may not feel the sting of the Father's discipline. Christ-followers who choose the path of sin will find that, ultimately, they will carry a double weight of pain: first, the pain of the inescapable consequences of their sin and, second, the pain of God's loving discipline in bringing them back to Him.

Why do Christ-followers sin?

The words of Paul in Ephesians 4:17-19 push us back to the question: Why do Christ-followers sin?

Sin defined

First, let's be clear about what 'sin' is. The theologians of the past have given us a great definition: 'Sin is any want of conformity unto, or transgression of, the law of God.'

You may recognize that as the answer to question 14 in the Westminster Shorter Catechism: 'What is sin?' But whether you memorized it as a child, or have read it for the first time here, it's an important statement and bears careful inspection. It correctly defines 'sin' in the following ways.

1. Sin is fundamentally rebellion against God Himself. We sometimes let ourselves minimize sin by believing that it is just the inevitable mistakes we humans make in relation to one another. This leads us to think of ourselves as pretty good if we make fewer of these mistakes than others do. In fact, we actually can get the idea that we're essentially good, and probably even worthy of heaven, as long as we measure our sinfulness on the scale of average human decency. But this is not reality.

Sin is, first and foremost, the wilful decision to go against what God commands of us. If that doesn't help you understand the utter vileness of sin, then just remember the penalty of sin – any sin, and every sin – is death. Whether we agree or not, in God's economy the penalty fits the crime. That means that sin – any sin, and every sin – is bad; really bad; really, really bad. Sin is bad because God is so good. It is essential to realize that when we look Him in the eye and defiantly go against His standards, we are committing a cosmic-sized crime.

2. We sin by *not* doing what God wants, as well as by *doing* what He forbids. The Westminster statement above captures this idea even if the old language needs updating. We sin when we refuse to do what God says is good, as well as when we decide to do what He says is bad.

We could summarize all this by referring to Romans 3:23, where Paul defined sin simply as falling 'short of the glory of God'. Sin is failing to live in alignment with God's requests and commands, and since Adam and Eve first chose to rebel against God, all of their descendants have been plagued with the presence, power, and penalty of sin.

Sin dissected

Now that we know what sin *is*, the question is *why do we do it?* Why would we risk offending the Almighty? Even more, why would we who love God the Father act in ways that make Him sad? Why would we pursue those things that Jesus died to free us from? All of these questions take us further toward the heart of the matter and help us come to a necessary, but humbling, admission: As Christ-followers, we no longer sin because we have to; we sin because we want to! And certainly, this needs some explaining.

Here's what we know from the Bible. Everyone comes into this world with a virus in their personal operating system called sin. We inherited this sin from Adam and Eve, and the absolute consequence of having it is that we all sin, just like Paul said in Romans 3:23: '... *for all have sinned and fall short of the glory of God'*. This virus continues to replicate itself in us – and for that matter, in all of creation – so that it permeates every corner of our being, influencing and corrupting our will, our intellect, our emotions, and even our physical bodies. Everywhere we turn, we will find that sin and its corrosive properties are having disastrous effects on our lives and world. (If you want a short description of how this all works, just read Romans 1:18-32 which seems to chronicle the steady decline of society as sin spreads its influence.)

All this means that, left to themselves, people sin. If God does nothing to fix the virus, everyone continues acting in accordance with it, and they sin. Theologians call this the problem of original sin, and the Bible is clear that it is as much a part of the spiritual DNA of sinful humanity as any physical chromosome. Simply put, humankind in its natural state of rebellion against God sins naturally. They sin, just like they breathe, as a function of who they are. While this does not mean that everyone acts as sinfully as possible, it does mean that ultimately, even one's best deeds and thoughts fall short of God's standards because they arise from a heart that is permeated with self-righteousness and a refusal to humble itself under the mighty hand of God. To God, even our 'righteous deeds' are just so many filthy garments (Isa. 64:6).

I know what you're thinking: Okay, so unbelievers sin by nature; but what about those of us who follow Christ? Aren't we supposed to be 'new creatures?' Don't we have a new nature? So, why do we still sin?

Good questions! And at this point I want to cut to the chase, without going all the way around the theological barn. Simply put, as Christ-followers we don't sin because we have to; we sin because we choose to. We sin because we want to!

At this point I expect that you have some objections. Like me, if asked you would certainly say you don't want to sin, that sin is a bad choice, and that you'd love to move as far away from it as you can. But if we look carefully at our lives, at the various decision points of our day, we'll have to admit that at crucial times we do choose sin over obedience simply because we want to. While this may not apply to every sin in our lives, it certainly does account for a huge portion of those sinful thoughts and practices that are responsible for making us look like those around us who don't love Jesus.

As Christ-followers, we've been given a new operating system. Paul describes this as Christ living in us (Gal. 2:20) which accounts for that fact that while our physical bodies are in decay, that which we really are – children of God – is being renewed, and progressively fitted for eternity (2 Cor. 4:16-18). We are described as a sample of God's new creation (2 Cor. 5:17) and as having been given the indwelling presence of God the Spirit (Rom. 8:9-11; Eph. 1:13, 14) and the mind of Christ (1 Cor. 2:16). As a result, we never encounter temptations that are irresistible (1 Cor. 10:13), and we are rightly called by God the Father to exhibit the family trait of holiness (1 Pet. 1:14, 15). Finally, God Himself has guaranteed that the process by which He is making us more and more like Christ will progress to its intended conclusion despite all the opposition Satan and this world throws up against it (Phil. 1:6; Jude 24). Given all this, not one Christ-follower – one in whom God the Spirit dwells – can say that they have to sin, that they have no recourse against the temptations of this world, or that they are powerless in their fight against sin and its deceitful call away from the heart of their Heavenly Father.

Once we come to own the truth that our sin stems from our own will, from our own decision to rebel against God, we're faced with the next crucial question: Why do we want to sin? What drives us to go against what we actually know is right and best?

This question has a two-part answer. First, we underestimate the effects of sin, and second, we overestimate the benefits of sin. Basically, we allow ourselves to believe that the upside of sin is huge, while its downside is negligible. Usually, therefore, by the time we recognize that we've believed our own lie, it's too late.

The effects of sin

At the heart of sin's genius is its ability to *deceive*. Sin first masqueraded as a beautiful fruit that promised a God-like understanding of right and wrong in the world. By the time Adam and Eve knew the truth, it was too late.

Everyday we are faced with the reality that sin disguises itself as life when it really is death. The fact that sin offers some immediate pleasure is usually enough to blind us to the mountain of pain lying just below reality's waterline. The first effect of sin is that it deceives us as to its reality and the inescapable consequences. It seems that we never grow to the place where sin's deceptive abilities no longer pose a danger. The writer of Hebrews passionately warns his readers: 'But encourage one another day after day, as long as it is still called "Today", so that none of you will be hardened by the deceitfulness of sin' (3:13).

Not only does sin *deceive*, sin *desensitizes*. Have you ever noticed that when you allow little sins to find a home in your mind or life that they make it easier for you to go even further down the pathway of sin? Maybe sin is like the mosquito that first injects some numbing chemical into our skin so we don't feel it when they start sucking out our blood. In the same way, sin blinds us to its heinous and progressive agenda, while desensitizing our hearts to the promptings and perceptions of the indwelling Spirit of God.

Lastly, sin *destroys*. Yes, it does. Sin is an agent of decay, and wherever it is allowed to sit and stay, it will begin to tear things apart. Sin never fixes things; sin always fractures things. Because sin also is the master of disguise, you probably won't recognize the destruction until it is too late to escape its consequences. Apparently, sin is very patient and is content to take territory a little at a time. In this way, through incremental advances, what entered as an invited guest through our decision to sin, becomes a tyrant while we aren't looking.

The mechanics of sin

I know what you're thinking. You're thinking that I've oversold the case, that I've painted a picture of sin with too broad a brush, that sin isn't really as explosively dangerous as I've made it out to be. Well let's see what the Bible has to say.

In the letter of James, the author – Jesus' half-brother – is apparently responding to an idea in the mind of his readers that they could pass off their sin as somehow God's doing. After all, if they fell to temptation, wasn't God to blame for allowing them to face it in the first place? Here's what James says:

> Blessed is a man who perseveres under trial; for once he has been approved, he will receive the crown of life which the Lord has promised to those who love Him. Let no one say when he is tempted, 'I am being tempted by God'; for God cannot be tempted by evil, and He Himself does not tempt anyone. But each one is tempted when he is carried away and enticed by his own lust. Then when lust has conceived, it gives birth to sin; and when sin is

accomplished, it brings forth death. Do not be deceived, my beloved brethren. (James 1:12-16)

James starts this section with a call to recognize that true blessing – the happy satisfaction of the soul – is found by those who resist temptation. He ends it with a call to his readers that they not be deceived. Deceived by what? Simply this: James doesn't want his readers to believe that somehow sin can bring blessing, that somehow their sin is part of what God is doing in their lives.

In verse 13 he declares that they can in no way lay their sin to God's account. While we could take pages to delve into what else this verse means, for our purposes here we need only understand that the full responsibility for our sin and its consequences lies with us, not God.

Verse 14 walks us through the mechanics of sin. It all starts with something outside of us ('tempted') that we choose to use as a vehicle for our own lusts ('carried away and enticed'). In King David's case, it was a beautiful young woman (see Appendix 1: 'How To Ruin Your Life'). In our lives it could be almost anything that we allow to awaken the sinful desires of our unredeemed flesh. When we allow our lusts to take flight on the wings of temptation, it is sin. Read it: 'when lust has conceived, it gives birth to sin …'

But notice that the process doesn't end there! Oh, we wish it would, don't we? We actually talk ourselves into believing that it ends there. We believe that we can sin, just a little, and experience the pleasure but not the pain; we simply don't think that sin is sinful.

The text goes on to say that sin always brings with it the unintended consequences of death. By that James means that sin is an agent of death, decay and destruction. Again, sin never fixes. Sin always destroys. It does so in disguise, incrementally, and brings forth death. James begged his readers not to be deceived into thinking any differently, and his message is just as necessary today.

Faith – an agent of true life

The mechanics of faith

The same author who so concisely described the way sin works had previously described the opposite side of the coin. Just as sin is the agent of death in those who choose it, so also those who choose to persevere in righteousness will find that their faith is an agent of true life, with all the satisfaction and joy that it brings. Here is what James says:

> Consider it all joy, my brethren, when you encounter various trials, knowing that the testing of your faith produces endurance. And let endurance have its perfect result, so that you may be perfect and complete, lacking in nothing. (James 1:2-4)

As in 1:12, James is talking about the joys of perseverance in righteousness. There he details the plight of those who don't persevere, who choose to give up and give in to sin. Here he details the delights that are found by those whose faith is tested, and stands up to the test. Like the muscle that is tested in the weight room, faith that perseveres grows stronger and stronger, enabling the soul to enjoy a complete joy, a satisfying alignment with the loving heart of God Himself.

In simple terms, the choices we make everyday as Christ-followers mirror these two texts from the pen of James. We all encounter opportunities to allow our lusts to take flight. How do we respond? In faith? Or in sin?

Two roads diverged

I still remember the Robert Frost poem 'The Road Not Taken' that I memorized as a child. It had a profound effect on me then, and it still provides me a powerful image, useful in the decision points of my day. Here's how.

In the poem, Frost places the reader at the place where the road he is travelling splits off into two roads, each heading a different direction. He looks down each road, trying to determine which offers the better experience. I find this a helpful visual for the many decision points each Christ-follower faces every day.

Let's say that I encounter a temptation, an opportunity to sin. It could be as big as the lion of sexual lust, or as small as the lizard of laziness. (Feel free to substitute your own temptations into this illustration.) And so I come to a decision point. First, I take a good, long look down the road of disobedience. It looks great! Everything I see appeals to me, and promises immediate satisfaction. It doesn't appear to have many risks, and those I do see can be pretty easily managed.

Then I look down the road of obedience to God, and frankly, it looks hard. It doesn't appear to offer any great excitement, and actually looks like it will require quite a bit of work on my part. Also, it doesn't at first seem to be going the direction I really want to go. So I stand, looking, trying to figure out which way to go. Do I persevere in righteousness, or do I give in to temptation and sin?

At this point, I hope you're tracking with me. We've seen that our blessed God is worthy of our complete trust. Further, we've seen that, in Christ, God the Father has sculpted us into a masterpiece of His grace. Now we've also agreed with the horrible truth that, as God's masterpieces, we still sin, and even worse, we do so because we – at some level – want to. We've come to embrace that every day we face the choice to sin, and that we often forget the utter sinfulness of sin, while undervaluing the joy and satisfaction that comes from walking in righteousness and truth. So now we stand looking down two roads, and feel the almost irresistible pull of sin to believe its lies and come looking for its pleasures. What can we do?

An answer

The scenario painted in the preceding paragraph is no different from the way Paul envisioned the life of faith. In Colossians 1:13 Paul says that we've been 'rescued … from the domain of darkness, and transferred … into the kingdom of His beloved Son'. In Christ, we're not who we used to be, and we don't live where we used to live. We've been rescued out of the bondage of sin (the domain of darkness) and now are privileged to live as citizens of the kingdom of God. But Paul doesn't stop there.

In Ephesians 6:13-17, Paul declares that we are given the armour of the Spirit for the very purpose of going back into the domain of darkness, now as agents of rescue. Wow! Not only are we to walk in righteousness, we are to do so in the middle of a world that is permeated by sin in all of its complexity. How can we possibly be expected to live for God in the middle of a world of sin?

I remember preaching this passage some years ago and really wrestling with the whole concept of standing firm. Paul states that the whole purpose of the armour is for the Christ-follower – in the midst of a depraved, sin-drenched world – to 'resist in the evil day, and having done everything, to stand firm'. The goal is not just to wear the armour, or even to enter the war. The goal is to stand firm against the swirling temptations of lust, greed, pride, laziness, anger, and a whole host of other things found in Satan's arsenal.

While all of the pieces of armour are worthy of their own book, my attention here is drawn to the shield of faith described in verse 16: '… in addition to all, taking up the shield of faith with which you will be able to extinguish all the flaming arrows of the evil one'.

Really? Is Paul telling the truth here? Is he really saying that somehow 'faith' can so shield the soul that the fire-carrying arrows of Satan can be extinguished before they enflame the lusts that still reside in our unredeemed bodies? Yes, Paul is telling us that faith – rightly understood, strengthened and maintained – can overwhelm temptation, allowing us to see through sin's deception, to evade its de-sensitizing effects, and to replace its destruction with the satisfying delights of obedience. We can come to the place where we choose the road of obedience, and come to experience its true joy. While 'faith' is a word we use so much that we may no longer really understand it, when we come to truly understand its power, we find that faith is the answer.

CHAPTER 5

Closing the gap

BEFORE heading on, let's look at where we've come. The almighty God, whose sovereignty and inerrant love has reached to us in forgiveness through Jesus Christ, has not only rescued us from sin but has also crafted us into masterpieces of His grace. We are meant to be His samples, His intentional masterworks, through which His greatness can shine into the darkness of a watching world. Wow!

But we've also had to admit that, as those who are following Christ, we still sin. What's more, we've come to own the awful truth that our sinful thoughts and actions are the result of our own selfish choices. As new creatures in Christ, we don't *have* to sin; we *choose* to sin.

The deathly gap

So there is this horrible, yet undeniable, gap between *who* we are in Christ, and *how* we so often live. This gap showed up in the lives of the Ephesians (remember Eph. 4:17?) and all too often is glaringly apparent in our lives, as well. We who have been delivered from the penalty of sin still choose to walk in it, and we make this choice far too often and much too easily.

Paul understands

In his letter to the Romans, chapter 7, Paul is crying out that he feels the gap. As a Christ-follower, he wants to live in holiness and truth, but the reality is that he doesn't do so consistently. What he wants as a Christ-follower is in conflict with what rages in his flesh. It is this 'law of sin' in his flesh (7:23) that too often wins the battle and moves his will to pursue that which he knows goes against God's law. He ends his description of his internal battle with a cry for help: 'Wretched man that I am! Who will set me free from the body of this death?' (7:24). What he is saying is just this: How is it possible to say 'no' to the desires of the flesh and 'yes' to the desires of the Spirit who dwells in me?

I think this is the fundamental question every Christ-follower asks repeatedly. If you're sincere in wanting to shine as God's masterpiece in a consistent and holy way, then you've been asked this question many times and many ways: 'How can I overwhelm the sinful passions that lurk in my as yet unredeemed flesh and which are hyper-sensitive to the temptations of this world, so that I can come to prefer the obedience God calls me to and the joy that accompanies it?' Paul was asking it, too, so we're in good company. Paul even supplies the answer he had already come to own: 'Thanks be to God through Jesus Christ our Lord!' (7:25). God's provision for us, in Jesus Christ, is the answer, but we'll have to let Paul give us the specifics.

The shield of faith

As we saw at the close of the last chapter, Paul saw the 'shield of faith' as a crucial element in his quest to ward of temptation and the sin it attempted to fuel. Remember? He wrote: ' … in addition to all, taking up the shield of faith with which you will be able to extinguish all the flaming arrows of the evil one' (Eph. 6:16). Paul saw in faith an answer to the problem of temptation. A strong and robust belief in the blessedness of God and the privilege of eternal life in Christ can provide the spiritual discernment necessary to see through the façade of sin's deception and recognize that what God offers through obedience is always better by far. That's what the writer of the letter to the Hebrews was trying to get across in one of the most important sections of the Bible dealing with the issues of faith and holy living. Let's look at it.

The race of faith

The author of Hebrews was deeply concerned that his readers not give in to the temptations that surrounded them. He likened the challenge of living for Christ in the midst of a broken world to a marathon, and like a great coach, he called them to keep running, to keep striving, all the way to the finish:

> Therefore, since we have so great a cloud of witnesses surrounding us, let us also lay aside every encumbrance and the sin which so easily entangles us, and let us run with endurance the race that is set before us, fixing our eyes on Jesus, the author and perfecter of faith, who for the joy set before Him endured the cross, despising the shame, and has sat down at the right hand of the throne of God. For consider Him who has endured such hostility by sinners against Himself, so that you will not grow weary and lose heart. (Heb. 12:1-3)

I need you to notice some things in this section:

First, understand that every Christ-follower has a race to run and it is hard and long and there are daily temptations that call us to give up and quit.

Second, the way to keep running, fighting off the temptations to quit, is to focus on Jesus Christ, who is called the 'author and perfecter of faith'.

What do we do with this? We understand that this race is a metaphor for the life of holiness that we've begun as Christ-followers. It is the call of Christ to follow Him, saying 'no' to the sinful desires of the flesh and 'yes' to the call of the indwelling Spirit of God to walk in holiness and truth. As Christ-followers we understand that this is, in reality, a spiritual, life-long marathon.

God, however, has not just asked us to run the race. He has also provided a way for us to fend off the desires of the flesh and the temptations of the world that enflame them. This provision is faith in Jesus Christ.

At this point I know that you're a bit disappointed because you've heard about faith before, you're sure you understand it, and you're certain that the faith you understand can't help you resist the overwhelming urges to sin that you've come to accept in your life. You were hoping for so much more, for some magic formula that would help you become more consistent in resisting temptations. But in spite of all that, I'm asking you to take a new look at what faith really is in the life of the Christ-follower. So let's head back to the letter to the Hebrews.

What is faith?

In Hebrews 10, the author recognizes that his readers are going through very rough times. If we read verses 19-25 carefully, we can understand that the pressures and temptations that surrounded them were starting to erode their confidence that following Christ was really worth it. They had begun to question the necessity of their doctrinal beliefs (10:23), the benefit of being part of the congregational gatherings (10:25) and, perhaps most importantly, the reality of their call to be and to live holy (10:22). The author has to coach them along this part of the race, reminding them that what God has done for them and is asking of them is their very best option.

He follows up these reminders with a sobering declaration that, in a way, each one of them was standing at a decision point, looking at the two roads that lay before them. The first road –

the road of wilful sin (10:26, 39a) – was headed for destruction and terrifying judgment in the hands of the living God (10:31). The other road – the road of enduring faith – would lead to great reward (10:35) and the preserving of the soul (10:39b).

Notice how he defines this 'faith to the preserving of the soul' (10:39). It is knowledge of a 'better possession' (10:34), a 'confidence' (10:35), 'endurance' (10:36), and the opposite of shrinking back (10:38). And if that isn't enough, he comes right out in 11:1 and defines this faith for us:

> Now faith is the assurance of things hoped for, the conviction of things not seen.

Putting this all together, we come to see that faith is not merely some opinion, or even a belief that something is true. It is more than that: it's an enduring confidence; a settled conviction; a radical assurance concerning Jesus Christ and the truth of the gospel message that keeps the soul from shrinking back, from giving up and from giving in.

But the author of Hebrews isn't done. Look at the last bit of information he gives us about this faith in 11:6:

> And without faith it is impossible to please Him, for he who comes to God must believe that He is and that He is a rewarder of those who seek Him.

Let's try and put it all together. First, getting faith right is pretty important because without it, it is impossible to please God. If you want to please God, you've got to be right about faith. Second, faith is an assurance, a conviction, a settled confidence. It is more than mere agreement with historical facts or doctrines. It is more than acceptance of some denominational distinctives or appreciation of the role of the church in society. Third, the content of this assurance, conviction, and confidence has everything to do with *who God is* ('must believe that He is') and *what He gives to those who seek Him* ('that He is a rewarder of those who seek Him').

Faith is the settled assurance that God is right in the way He has described Himself in the Bible, combined with a radical determination that all He has for those who seek Him is worth everything my life has to give Him.

Over the years I have come to see in the following definition a helpful understanding of faith:

> Faith is ... a life-dominating conviction that all God has for me through obedience is better by far than anything this world or Satan offers me through selfishness and sin.

Remember the two roads? When we look down the road of sin, it appears pleasing, exciting and easy, while the road of obedience can look daunting, and even appear not to be heading in the direction we think we want to travel. It is at this point that faith has to make the difference. We really have to be convinced that whatever God has for us down the road of obedience is not merely *as good* but actually *better by far* than what we'll find down the road of sin. As we tear the above definition of faith apart, we'll come to see the place faith can play and also the necessity of building a life-dominating faith that is strong enough to overwhelm the powerful, sinful passions that still remain in our flesh.

But before doing that, there's one more thing we need to understand about faith.

First faith

If you're tracking with me, you've begun to see where we're headed. You're probably sensing that the only way to overwhelm sin is with a greater appreciation for what God has for us through obedience. If so, you're on the right track! But before we can go on to talk about this kind of strong, enduring, life-dominating faith, we first have to be sure we know where faith comes from, and how it grows.

The Bible is clear that faith is not something that we just work up. In fact, in the lives of those who are not yet following Christ, it is clear that faith as we've described it is actually impossible. Paul reminds us of this in 1 Corinthians 2:14:

> But a natural man does not accept the things of the Spirit of God, for they are foolishness to him; and he cannot understand them, because they are spiritually appraised.

The 'natural man' in this verse is the man or woman who is still at odds with God. Such people have been born with the toxin of sin in their very nature, inherited from Adam and Eve, and they are still living according to their own agenda and plan in rebellion against the God who created them. Paul says that, as long as folks are in this condition, the truths concerning God and Jesus Christ and all the rest will fall on their minds as just so much foolishness. While they may come to be curious about them or even find the facts and events of the Bible comforting, they will not be able to put all the pieces together and come to have saving faith.

Here we run into a great mystery. We've seen that without faith it is impossible to please God, yet we also know that faith can't be manufactured in the unbeliever's heart. Now that's a real problem!

The Bible is clear, however, that God Himself provides the solution. The faith that God requires, He gives. That's what Paul says in Ephesians 2:8: 'For by grace you have been saved through faith; and that not of yourselves, it is the gift of God ...'

It is clear from the grammar of Paul's original Greek sentence that the 'gift of God' refers to *both* the grace that saves and the faith through which saving grace is experienced. Paul's whole point is that the rescue God carries out on our behalf is completely His doing. He gives us salvation in its entirety, including the faith by which we accept it.

This is what I call 'first faith'. It is a gift to us from God, which comes to us as God the Spirit rides into our minds on the wings of the gospel. He opens our deaf spiritual ears and blind spiritual eyes to the truth of our sin and, as well, to Christ's loving offer of forgiveness. We turn from the sin and turn to the Saviour, and we are granted all the benefits of the death and righteousness of Christ. What an amazing transaction!

This 'first faith' fits well into the definition above. When the Spirit opens our eyes to our sinfulness and then to the prospect of forgiveness and new life in Jesus Christ, faith says, 'Run to Jesus because what He has for you is better by far than anything your sinful existence could ever offer you!' God grants us this 'first faith' and, through it, His grace rescues us from sin and grants us standing in His family as sons and daughters.

Firm faith

But first faith was meant to grow increasingly into firm faith. This fundamental spiritual truth is seldom grasped in today's world. We too often relegate 'faith' to that initial trust in Christ and leave it at that. Somehow we understand that we 'came by faith' to rest in Jesus but have forgotten that we are called as well to 'live by faith'. That is, we are to understand that in order to grow strong in Christ and ward off temptation and sin, our first faith has to be strengthened and enlarged, increasingly growing into a firm, unshakeable faith.

The idea that we can have faith and still be expected to grow that faith is seen in several places in the Bible. Can you identify with the man in Mark 9:24 who, after asking Jesus to heal his son, cried out, 'I do believe; help my unbelief'? I can – and I also resonate with the Lord's disciples as they heard Him teach on forgiveness, insisting that His followers forgive the same person 490 times: 'Increase our faith!' (Luke 17:5).

The truth is undeniable that what Christ asks of us will demand more than first faith; it will require a deep and settled assurance as to His credibility and a radical trust that what He promises for us down the road of obedience *has no equal* in the realm of rebellion and sin.

Paul knew this, and when he brought the gospel to the Gentile world, he insisted that those who turned to Christ did not settle for faith in its beginning stages, even though it brought them into the family of God. To the Corinthian believers he said it this way:

> For we are not overextending ourselves, as if we did not reach to you, for we were the first to come even as far as you in the gospel of Christ; not boasting beyond our measure, that is, in other men's labours, but with the hope that *as your faith grows,* we will be, within our sphere, enlarged even more by you. (2 Cor. 10:14-15, emphasis added)

Also, in writing to the Thessalonian believers, he greeted them by saying:

> We ought always to give thanks to God for you, brethren, as is only fitting, because *your faith is greatly enlarged,* and the love of each one of you toward one another grows ever greater. (2 Thess. 1:3, emphasis added)

Putting it together

We've seen that, as Christ-followers, there is too often a gap between who God has made us to be in Christ and how we live. We've also seen that when faith is rightly understood as a powerful conviction concerning the reality of almighty God, and the rewards He offers to those that diligently obey Him, it provides a powerful protection to the soul against the onslaught of Satan's temptations. It becomes a shield around the heart and mind, that if properly strengthened and maintained, can 'extinguish all the flaming arrows of the evil one' (Eph. 6:16). This is what I've come to call *the obedience option.* It is choosing the best from among the many choices, many of them sinful.

It is standing at the place of decision, looking down the two roads, and preferring what God has for you down the path of righteousness. When you choose the obedience option you will find that the rewards truly are better by far.

Now it's time to re-examine our definition of faith, pulling it apart so that we can begin to grow a firm, shield-like faith. We'll do this in the next chapter and then discuss how to grow such a faith in chapters 7 and 8.

CHAPTER 6

The faith that shields

L ET'S take a look at the definition of faith that I've suggested, and tear it apart so that we can understand just what a shielding faith looks like. As we do, we'll begin to understand more fully the power of the obedience option.

A definition of faith

> Faith is ... *a life-dominating conviction* that all God has for me through obedience is better by far than anything this world or Satan offers me through selfishness and sin.

A life-dominating conviction

At the very beginning of this understanding of faith is the idea that faith has to be *the* dominating principle of your life. Jesus Christ never called us to halfway faith; His call was plainly to an 'all in' faith. He made it clear in Luke 9:23: 'And He was saying to them all, 'If anyone wishes to come after Me, he must deny himself, and take up his cross daily and follow Me.'

If you and I want to live in ways that are increasingly holy and faithful to Christ, that more and more resist temptation, and less and less give in to sin, we have to give ourselves every day to this proposition, declared by Paul in Galatians 2:20:

> I have been crucified with Christ; and it is no longer I who live, but Christ lives in me; and the life which I now live in the flesh *I live by faith* in the Son of God, who loved me and gave Himself up for me. (emphasis added)

You and I must understand this. We must recognize and gladly acknowledge what Paul is saying. To follow Christ means to admit that who I was and the way I lived were self-destructive and dangerous. I was walking the path to death and judgment, and living with their down payment all the while. My joy was shallow and short-lived, and my greatest fears arose from the certainty that I could neither fix myself nor change the tragic trajectory of my life. It was then I met Jesus. As Paul explains, He breathed new life into me and made me a new person. That means that the life I am now living is actually His and my greatest joy will be found in living His life in ways that testify to His greatness and validate His wise commands.

To follow Jesus Christ is to acknowledge joyfully that He now has me, completely, and that whatever He asks of me is my very best option. This becomes the essential foundation of my worldview. It is *the* conviction that dominates everything else in my life.

Faith is … a life-dominating conviction *that all God has for me through obedience* is better by far than anything this world or Satan offers me through selfishness and sin.

All God has for me through obedience

Imagine that you're staring down the two roads again. What do you see? If you look through the eyes of firm faith, you'll see that the writer to the Hebrews was right: God 'is a rewarder of them that diligently seek him' (Heb. 11:6, KJV). What God has for each of us down the daily road of obedience to Him is simply amazing.

Have you ever taken the time to think about the rewards of obedience? While our minds are bombarded daily with the 'pleasures' that sin promises, we hardly ever contemplate what God promises to those who choose the obedience option. This might be the reason we think the road of disobedience so often looks like the better deal! While it would go beyond the scope of this book to trace all of the 'rewards' God has for those who obey, here are a few of the more significant ones:

- Proverbs 3:5-6: If we don't lean on our own skewed understanding, but rather trust fully in the Lord, He will make our 'paths straight'; that is, He will so guide the affairs of our lives that we will, in the end, look back to see that we travelled the best route and arrived at the very best destination.

- Psalm 84:11: God promises that He will not withhold that which He knows is truly good from those whose lives are aligned with His commands.

- Joshua 1:8: Joshua was promised that adherence to the law of God and a growing and consistent commitment to it would ensure that his life would be one of success and prosperity as defined by God Himself.

- James 1:12: God promises that those who persevere in righteousness during times of great testing, will be given the 'crown of life'. This reward speaks not only to the eternal duration of life in Christ, but also to the fact that those who obey God find a level of true living in this world that satisfies without regret.

- Psalm 28:7: Those who trust in the Lord will find Him to be the source of a strength that this world can neither give nor explain.

- Psalm 16:11: Perhaps the greatest reward God gives to those who follow Him in obedience is the presence of joy. What our hearts long for and our days are spent pursuing is, ultimately, found only in the presence of God Himself.

If we add to this all that flows from the metaphor God Himself has chosen to define His relationship to us – loving Father – we'll find that every conceivable delight that we could ask for is available from His loving hand. He grants us: joy and peace; understanding and patience; the love of family; the strength to endure trial; the courage to resist evil; the fellowship of the saints; the mutual care of the church; the knowledge of the Scriptures; the privilege of prayer; the opportunity to transform lives and society through the gospel; the assurance of His guaranteed provision for both life and godliness; the comfort of the indwelling Spirit; the certainty of heaven; and so on and on. All of this and more is wrapped up in the euphoria of obedience as we steadfastly resist sin and diligently seek Him.

Lastly, we could add as one of the greatest rewards, the fact that on the road of obedience there are no sin-caused consequences, no humiliating spiritual scars, no fatherly discipline, no shame, no guilt – no regrets.

> Faith is ... a life-dominating conviction that all God has for me through *obedience is better by far* than anything this world or Satan offers me through selfishness and sin.

Obedience is better by far

In my experience, we all play the game of weighing out our options. Which one offers the better return? Which one carries the greater risk? I'll admit I certainly have done that when confronted with the opportunity to sin. It might go like this: 'Is the sin really that bad? Can I get away with it? What's the worst thing that can happen?' And on and on. When I begin to compare the pleasures of sin with the rewards of obedience, I could consider it this way: 'Okay, I suppose I could say "no" to sin and "yes" to obedience, but then how do I feel? Frankly, sin offers some excitement, but obedience – well, there's no excitement there!'

Can you resonate with that? Have you ever thought that obedience just doesn't offer anything real, tangible and worth fighting for? Have you even got to the place where you've determined that, as a Christ-follower guaranteed to enter heaven, you've already gained all the 'rewards' possible and there's no compelling reason to be consistently obedient to Christ in the meantime? Well, its time to think again!

If you took the time to read through and reflect on the rather short list of 'rewards' on the previous page – the things that God has for you through obedience – you certainly would have come to the conclusion that what God has for you today, tomorrow and every day is not merely a good feeling; nor is it on par with what sin offers; nor is it just marginally better than the pleasures sin promises (but actually fails to deliver). In reality, sin *offers you nothing good!* Remember, sin is an agent of destruction. Sin never fixes things; sin only destroys them. When you factor in the consequences of sin (see ch. 4), you must admit that sin is really a bad deal. It claims to offer maximum pleasure at a minimum price but actually delivers nothing of value while extracting a high cost in the end.

All this adds up to the truth that the obedience option really is better by far. What God has for us through obedience is always *better by far* than what you can gain through sin in all of its deceptive forms. Think of it this way. Shame or honour? Death or life? Regret or joy? God's discipline or His blessing?

As we stand at each decision point in our day looking down the two roads, the strength of our faith will make the difference.

> Faith is … a life-dominating conviction that all God has for me through obedience is better by far *than anything this world or Satan offers me through selfishness and sin.*

Than anything this world or Satan offers me through selfishness and sin

I want to be fair here. Satan, and the world system he has co-opted, do claim to have quite a bit to offer. His storehouse of 'pleasures' is filled and overflowing. He has masterfully duplicated almost all of the things God has graciously provided for our wellbeing. He has re-defined love as lust, success as accumulation, and wealth as monetary, while convincing us that selfishness is a right, humility a weakness, and integrity a poor business decision. He has manufactured all the opportunities we could ever want to have our own way, to go for the gusto and to love the one we're with – seemingly without consequence. Satan makes sin so easy, and so inviting. No wonder it is so hard to see through the façade. We make it even harder when we start looking, not through the lens of faith, but through the lens of our desire for immediate gratification.

But never forget it is all a lie, especially for the Christ-follower. If you have turned from your sin to follow Jesus Christ, you're not who you used to be. You're His masterpiece, living His life, through the power of the indwelling Spirit of God. What's more, the things from Satan's storehouse that once appealed to you can actually be seen by you for what they really are: agents of death! Paul makes a point of this to the Philippian believers. He prays that, as their love for Christ grows, they will become more and more perceptive in assessing the spiritual value of the choices before them:

And this I pray, that your love may abound still more and more in real knowledge and all discernment, *so that you may approve the things that are excellent*, in order to be sincere and blameless until the day of Christ. (Phil. 1:9-10, emphasis added)

One of the greatest benefits of a strong, growing, overwhelming faith is that, through our deepening conviction as to the reality of who God is and how He works, it allows us to see through sin's deceptive façade. Paul prays that the Philippians would grow to the place where they will be able to discern, from among all the options before them, the 'things that are excellent'.

Let me use an illustration that might make the obedience option more clear. Let's imagine a business man – a Christ-follower with a wife and kids – is on a business trip that takes him away from home for six days. During his return home, he's stuck in an unfamiliar airport for several hours waiting for a connecting flight. He's tired and misses his family, and frankly, is in a place of spiritual susceptibility. He strolls past the news and magazine outlet and knows that there are some soft-porn magazines in there that would provide him with some excitement, some pleasure.

At first, he weighs the options. 'No one knows me here. I could totally get away with it. It wouldn't really be that bad. Lots of guys do it.' But as he starts down the road of disobedience, his firm faith starts to work. 'Wait a minute! Yes, those magazines do appeal to me, at least to part of me. They appeal to my flesh! But who I really am – a child of God – understands that they aren't what they appear to be. God's provision for my sexual satisfaction is my wonderful wife, with whom I've made a family! Those magazines are not life; they're really agents of death to me. They would make me dissatisfied with my wife, leave a residue of shame and guilt that would trigger anger, and most of all, giving in to this kind of sexual temptation is really just my way of saying God is wrong about sin, and can no longer be trusted to provide for all my needs! Nope, the rewards of obedience are a much better deal, and they come with no shame, no guilt, and no regret.' So he chooses the obedience option and as he keeps walking he begins to feel the euphoria of obedience. What he has in Christ is better by far than anything the world or Satan can offer through selfishness and sin.

An unbelieving believer

In the previous illustration, the business man looked through the lens of firm faith and affirmed that what God had for him through obedience really was better by far than anything the world or Satan could offer through selfishness and sin. But what if he had given in to the temptation and chosen the road of disobedience?

Imagine it's you. You're standing and looking down the two roads that are laid out before you. Suppose that, though a Christ-follower, you decide that the pleasures of sin are what you want, and you go down that road. Here's the best we can say about you at that point: You're an 'unbelieving believer'. That's right. You're now just like the folks Paul was addressing in Ephesians 4:17. Remember? He asked that they stop living like those who didn't know Jesus. That's you. You look and act just like those who don't believe. You haven't agreed with God about the sinfulness of sin, nor about the glories of grace, nor about the joy of following Jesus Christ! You've adopted the worldview of unbelief, determining that your own desires are more valuable to you than the divine offerings of almighty God. You've decided that sin should win over holiness, that Adam and Eve chose the better option, and that you're smarter than God.

The only problem is that you're wrong, and at some level you know it. Even as you thumb your nose at God, you're hoping He doesn't notice. While you're trying desperately to rationalize your sinful actions, who you really are – a redeemed child of the king – is trying to get you to want something better than sin. But you don't listen because at that point, your shield has been cast aside. Your faith in Christ has been overwhelmed and thrown down in favour of the passing pleasures of sin.

But if you stare down both roads and see sin as it really is, you'll recognize that it is death to you. With the same clear vision you'll see that the obedience option offers life and as you pursue righteousness an amazing thing will happen. You'll come to experience the joy – the absolute euphoria – that is found in fully trusting Jesus Christ to know what is best for you. You've given Him your life and what He can do with it through the obedience option truly is better, so much better, than what you can do with it through selfishness and sin. Count on it.

Now that we know the place and power of a firm, shield-like, overwhelming faith, let's consider how the Bible tells us such a faith can be grown, strengthened and maintained. That's what the next two chapters are all about.

CHAPTER SEVEN

Growing a faith that shields: Part 1

BACK in chapter 1, I told a true story about my interactions with a college athlete for whom lust had become an overwhelming enemy. If you remember, he told me that he felt powerless to resist when the opportunity for sexual gratification presented itself. I responded with a 'what if' that offered him cold, hard cash if he resisted sexual temptation. Not surprisingly, the 'irresistible' grip of sexual temptation suddenly became weak as his need for money overwhelmed it. What we both learned that day is this:

> The only way to overcome a desire for sin is to overwhelm it with a greater desire for righteousness.

Speaking truth in our hearts

Before going any further, I have to ask you this: Do you really want to grow a faith that shields you from temptation? Do you really want to turn away from sin? I ask this because we all know that sin brings pleasure. We can't deny that and to try to do so would be to lie to ourselves. Above all, we need to tell ourselves the truth.

In Psalm 15:1, the psalmist poses the big question: 'O LORD, who may abide in Your tent? Who may dwell on Your holy hill?' What he is really saying is this: What does the man or woman look like who really and truly wants to experience relationship with God, to 'live' with Him?

As we have seen, of course, there is risk involved here. A relationship with a holy God is not for the faint-hearted, especially if we have come to see our own weakness and ongoing struggle to prefer holiness over sin. That's the question you and I have to answer, even before we press on to build a shield-like faith: Do we want to live with God in close fellowship? Do we want to turn away from sin's pleasures? Do we really want to build an 'overwhelming' kind of faith?

For those who do, the psalmist answers the question in verse 2: 'He who walks with integrity, and works righteousness, and speaks truth in his heart.' You might say these are the Big Three: walking in integrity, working righteousness, and speaking truth in the heart. For now, I want to stress the third one: speaking truth in the heart.

You'll notice that it doesn't say speaking truth *from* the heart. Rather, the psalmist is stressing the necessity to speak truth *in* the heart. That means you have to tell yourself the truth. To pursue a way of life that enjoys the nearness of God, you and I first have to tell ourselves the truth about our desire for sin and about the benefits of righteousness. No more denials. No more rationalizations. No more excuses. Rather, there has to be a radical determination to understand, recognize, and pursue the great delights God holds out to those who love Him, who turn from sin to serve His glory, and who persevere in their pursuit of righteousness and the euphoria of obedience. We have to want clarity about the sinfulness of sin and the beauty of holiness. We have to commit to telling ourselves the truth.

Growing an overwhelming faith

I really don't like formulas. In fact, I mistrust those who give formulas as answers to tough questions and challenges. But on the other hand, I love simplicity. In my complex world, what I find helpful are what I call 'pointers'. These 'pointers' are simple sayings or symbols that point me back to deeper study I have done, reminding me of important conclusions I have come to and the righteous commitments I have made. My wedding ring is one of these. I'm looking at it right now, and it reminds me that, though my wonderful wife is out of town as I'm writing, our hearts are joined and our lives are not two but one. This little band of gold points me back to the joys we share and the commitments that increase and preserve them.

So at the risk of appearing to give a formula, I'm going to point you to 2 Timothy 2:22 as such a pointer – or rather a series of pointers – that I have found invaluable in growing a faith that can overwhelm temptation. Here it is.

> 'Now flee from youthful lusts and pursue righteousness, faith, love and peace, with those who call on the Lord from a pure heart.'

Before we dig into the rich truths of this verse, just take a moment to look at three important words: *Flee … pursue … with* …. I believe with all my heart that the life-long privilege of building a faith that shields my soul from temptation will consistently follow the pattern of these three words. They point me back to what I know to be true, to how I have committed myself to think and live, and to the joys I have experienced as a result. It is my prayer that they'll have the same benefit in your life. So, let's go!

'Flee'

Self-discipline

The first pointer is 'Flee'. The apostle Paul is writing to a relatively young man named Timothy. He has been left in Ephesus as a young pastor, charged with the task of leading there a fledgling group of Christ-followers. Paul recognizes that Timothy is at risk. The combination of Timothy's youth and the rampant wickedness of the Ephesian culture add up to great challenges for both Timothy and those he is shepherding. In fact, the whole letter is designed to encourage Timothy to be strong and courageous in the pastoral office assigned to him. He needs to live and lead well. Against the constant threat of personal, moral disqualification, Paul calls him to be a 'vessel for honour, sanctified, useful to the Master, prepared for every good work' (2 Tim. 2:21). On the heels of this call, Paul offers the command of verse 22. And he begins with 'Flee!'

Paul's point here is pretty clear: Timothy, run away from that which will enflame your lusts! This has long been the foundation of holy living. I put it in the category of *self-discipline*, which I define this way: Saying 'no' to my sinful desires. When temptations arise, or if I see something coming that will stoke the fire of any of my various lusts and sinful desires, I discipline myself to say 'no'. Self-discipline is saying 'no' to the desires of my as yet unredeemed flesh.

As a Christ-follower, Timothy realizes that saying 'yes' to the desires of the flesh will lead to sinful behaviour, and a loss of usefulness to the Master. Paul affirmed the necessity of self discipline this way in 1 Corinthians 9:27: '… but I discipline my body and make it my slave, so that, after I have preached to others, I myself will not be disqualified'.

Paul recognized that the simple starting point in any opposition to temptation and sin was the discipline of saying 'no' to the desires of the flesh. If left unchecked, these lusts will rule over you and even bring you to ruin. Paul's words to Timothy – and to us – are to make sure that his effectiveness in living and serving Christ is never hurt by giving in to the sinful impulses of the flesh.

We can't forget that our first duty in opposing sin and selfishness it to be hard on ourselves, to guard our hearts against the sinful desires that are present within us, and that are so susceptible to the things our society parades before us. It is very evident that the desire for that which God forbids seems to have come 'pre-installed' on our human hard drive. Proverbs 4:23 demands that we take proactive steps to shield our hearts and minds from those things that will pollute and enflame our lusts: 'Watch over your heart with all diligence, for from it flow the springs of life.' Later, in Colossians 3:5, Paul traced the sinful desires of the flesh all the way back to the bedrock of idolatry, demanding that we tell ourselves the truth: Our desire for that which God forbids is really our attempt to replace His authority with our agenda. Paul calls us to *flee* when we see those things coming that will fuel the lusts that still remain in our hearts.

Jesus also called us to an intentional denial of our sinful desires when He said in Luke 9:23, 'If anyone wishes to come after Me, let him deny himself, and take up his cross daily, and follow Me.' Commenting on this self denial, Alexander Whyte had this to say many years ago:

> Lay this down for a law, all my brethren, a new testament, and never to be abrogated law, that the best and safest religion for you is that way of religion that is hardest on your pride, and on your self-importance, on your self-esteem, as well as on your purse, and on your belly. You are not likely to err by practicing too much of the cross.'

There is a great danger, however, in self-discipline. Unfortunately too many Christ-followers have made self-discipline the main part of their strategy against sin. Their answer to the question of temptation is to rely on abstinence alone. In fact, some build their entire house of holy living on the foundation of what they don't do. They put together elaborate lists of 'don'ts' and then define their spirituality – and that of everyone around them – by the consistency with which they don't do the listed items.

The reality is that, while self-discipline is necessary, it simply isn't sufficient. Self-discipline can never accomplish the task of overcoming sin by itself. Self-discipline can help us avoid sin, but it can't help us build up righteousness. Self-discipline is an essential part of the whole, but it is simply ineffective by itself. Here's why: anyone can exhibit self-discipline. It isn't a fruit of the Spirit and takes no divine assistance. In fact, many of the most disciplined people in the world aren't Christ-followers at all. They have foolishly taken on severe lifestyles of rigorous self-discipline thinking that, by denying sinful desires, they could destroy them. But sinful desires are only overcome as they are replaced by an overwhelming desire for righteousness.

The great problem with self-discipline as the sole strategy against sin is that saying 'no' to the desires of the flesh does nothing to diminish those desires. In fact, as we've all experienced, saying 'no' may actually increase the intensity of the temptation.

Say you come home one day and the smell of freshly-baked, chocolate-chip, Macadamia nut cookies (my favourite!) meets you. You can almost taste them as they sit there on the counter, still hot, having just come out of the oven. You start to salivate and begin to imagine how the warm, gooey, nutty combo will feel and taste in your mouth. But then you remember you're trying to lose that weight around the middle. You summon up your courage and you say 'no' to the cookies and instead walk outside into the backyard. You've escaped temptation, but have you really diminished its power? No. You're outside physically, but in your mind, the taste and feel of the cookies persists. So you go back into the kitchen. Has your initial refusal to eat a cookie done anything to diminish the desire to eat one now? Maybe; but probably not. The only way you'll be able to overcome the desire to eat is by replacing it with a greater desire to persevere in your decision to cut out needless calories. So you start thinking about the benefits of sticking to your commitment, and as you do so, you find that the desire to eat – while not destroyed – is greatly diminished as your determination to stick to your diet grows.

Self-discipline is important, necessary, and a commanded component of our strategy against sin and temptation. But it isn't enough! It may win a battle, but it can never win the war.

Self-control

In contrast to self-discipline (which is saying 'no' to the desires of the flesh) I define self-control as saying 'yes' to the desires of the Spirit. While self-discipline is primarily centred on my will and fuelled by my determination (although in Christ-followers, the righteous desire to flee from sin is strengthened by the indwelling Spirit of God), self-control centres on God's will and is energized and directed by the Holy Spirit. Self-discipline focuses on binding and depriving fleshly desires while self-control focuses on replacing those desires with righteous ones.

Self-control primarily speaks of influences that bring power to direct the way I think and act. Paul includes self-control in the list of those fruits produced by the Holy Spirit as He takes up residence in our lives. But Paul's use of this term bears some closer study.

The Greek word (*ekpaths; ekpatais*) Paul uses in Galatians 5:23 to describe the last of the nine 'fruits of the Spirit' comes from the world of Greek and Hellenistic philosophy. It was used significantly in the writings of the ancient philosophers to speak of 'self-determinism'. They boasted in their personal 'autonomy', 'independence', and 'self-reliance'. They insisted that the greatest personal achievement was to become 'self-sustaining and self-governing'. It is no wonder this word is never found in the teaching of the Lord, or in the Gospels. The Greek understanding of 'self-control' was just the opposite of Christ's message of submission to the king of heaven. So when we encounter this word in Paul's writings, it is quite surprising. But a closer look clears it up.

When Paul uses 'self-control' he does so in light of his concept of the new self. As Paul states in Galatians 2:20, his old life was 'crucified with Christ' and he has now, in Christ, begun a new life that is actually the life of Christ being lived in him. Here's the verse:

> I have been crucified with Christ; and it is no longer I who live, but Christ lives in me; and the life which I now live in the flesh I live by faith in the Son of God, who loved me and gave Himself up for me.

Paul recognized that he was now the recipient of a new life, and that life as it was meant to be, was found only in Christ. The Spirit of God had taken up residence in him, and now self-control was really 'Spirit-control'. The old self had been crucified on the cross with Christ, and the Spirit had brought new life – a new self – that is being renewed and restored to the image of Christ Himself. It is this 'new self' that is to control the life of the believer. So by using the concept of self-control, Paul infuses a Greek concept with Christian meaning; the child of God, having the Spirit within, is thereby capable of the only righteous kind of self-control.

This self-control is focused, not so much on preventing sin, as on sustaining a righteous faith that produces holy living. It is to this idea of self-control that Paul turns in the second of the pointers in 2 Timothy 2:22.

'Pursue'

The second pointer is 'pursue'. I can still remember the first time this word actually made sense to me in this verse. My story is that I grew up in a religious setting where saying 'no' to the desires of the flesh was really the focus. Whether or not it was the intent of my parents and teachers, I came to believe that holy living was primarily about *not doing or thinking certain things*. My spiritual energy was all about defence! My spirituality was all about abstinence. While I am sure that I was encouraged to have an *offensive* plan to grow in knowledge and relationship with God, I was never shown the connection between the pursuit of righteousness and the ability to stay away from sin. I thought staying away from sin was all about my resolve. No one ever told me that it was much more about my passion for righteousness.

Perhaps it is too simple to say that the best direction to flee lusts is toward righteousness, but it's true. It's not enough to run away from sin; you and I must run to righteousness, and not only during times of temptation. The pursuit of righteousness is the daily privilege of every Christ-follower and the foundation for growing a shield-like faith.

In a following chapter we'll look at some ways that this pursuit of righteousness can become a real and satisfying experience. But, first, we have to get an overall idea of just what Paul is saying.

The first thing is to understand that 'pursue' is a very active word. Paul is calling us to an active and intentional chasing after that which is righteous in our world. It is a commitment of life to seek after those things that God loves and, as the necessary consequence, turn from and leave behind those things He hates. Never forget that the call of Christ on our lives is to follow, not sit. There is no such thing as couch-potato Christianity, even though many are attempting to follow Christ from the comfort of their own brand of recliner religion.

Let me take you back to my days at Pacific Lutheran University when I was privileged to work with many of the football players. I was deeply impressed with their diligence in the weight room. You have to know that PLU's philosophy of training was different from other places. The players were expected to get and to stay in shape on their own time. It was their shared commitment to excellence that made them intentional as individuals to run and lift, and do all the other things necessary to be successful on Saturday afternoons. I would often head to the weight room to find guys and spend time talking with them as they pushed themselves with higher weights and longer sets. They pushed themselves and endured the pain in order to be ready to withstand the violence of the game of football.

I can't imagine any of those guys deciding that they could skip the weight training week after week and still think they could have the strength to stop a 250 pound fullback with a full head of steam on Saturday. It would be ludicrous. But all too often we as Christ-followers think that we can withstand the challenges of our sin-drenched world without any real spiritual weight lifting. We foolishly think that flabby spiritual muscles are good enough to meet temptation and withstand its force.

The pursuit of righteousness begins with an intentional commitment to lift the spiritual weights of study, meditation, prayer, worship, service, stewardship, and proclamation. It is a pursuit that demands an ongoing desire to please God, oppose sin, and experience the joys that are promised to those who seek the Lord with all their heart.

Pursuing righteousness

We've already discussed that true faith is a life-dominating conviction that whatever God has for us through obedience is better by far than anything sin or Satan can offer through selfishness and sin. The pursuit of righteousness takes this seriously. The energy necessary to hit the spiritual weight room comes from an absolute conviction that we'll be better off for it; that the rewards of righteousness really are *better by far*; and that a growing knowledge of God, His Word and His ways will be its own reward, while still offering a better foundation for joyful living and a surer footing in the battle against sin and selfishness. Even more, as righteousness becomes more and more a passion in every area of your life, you'll find that the power of temptation is less and less. Your passion for righteousness will have the effect of decreasing your passion for sin and its deceptive offerings.

The pursuit of righteousness is the overarching mission of those who follow Christ, or at least it ought to be! In Hosea 14:9, the prophet recognized that this pursuit was to be the distinguishing characteristic of those who walk in wisdom:

> Whoever is wise, let him understand these things;
> Whoever is discerning, let him know them.
> For the ways of the LORD are right,
> And the righteous will walk in them,
> But transgressors will stumble in them.

The intentional pursuit of righteousness is the choice, every day, to know, understand, and walk in the ways of the Lord. What Hosea knew, and we need never forget, is that this is the wisest choice we have. The pursuit of righteousness is always our very best choice.

But just what does this pursuit look like in the context of meeting and resisting temptation? Simply this: In those moments when Satan starts slinging his fiery arrows of sin and selfishness at us, our only defence will be that we have developed and grown a passion for righteousness that is more powerful, more real, and certainly more satisfying than the increasing pressure to give in to the temptation. What Satan promises is really a lie; but what obedience to Christ in that moment offers will be seen as real and delightful to the extent that we have built up our knowledge of, and preference for, righteousness.

Let me use an example from the life of Joseph. You'll remember that, as a young boy, he was sold into slavery by his brothers and eventually ended up as a slave in the house of a prominent Egyptian named Potiphar. As the story unfolds in Exodus 39, Potiphar's wife takes quite a liking to this young Israelite man and offers him the opportunity to have sex with her. Just think about the situation: a teenage boy, living in a foreign country with no family support, confronted with the temptation of sexual fulfilment with the wife of his master. In the movies, this plot line always ends the same way – in bed – because these kinds of temptations are so powerful. But Joseph said 'no' and ran away.

The story of Joseph is important, but not only because he said 'no' to the desires of the flesh and fled. It is important because of the reasons that led to his courageous obedience. Long before he got into the situation with Potiphar's wife, Joseph had been busy in the pursuit of righteousness. When temptation hit like a sledgehammer, he was able to see it clearly as Satan's lie. He also was able to see clearly the fact that what God had for him through obedience was better by far. At the moment of crisis, his knowledge of God and His ways pulled the curtain of deception away from the opportunity, and he was able to see reality.

First, Joseph realized that what the woman was offering was hurtful to his master, who had placed great trust in him. Second, he realized that to engage in the offered wickedness would be to love evil and sin against God. And I know what you're thinking! How in the world does a teenage boy think of those things when a woman is standing in front of him offering sex? The answer is that long before this incident, and in ways that were intentional and consistent, Joseph had pursued righteousness. He had read and studied, reflected and prayed, and taken pains to fill his heart and head with the realities of God. By so doing, he was able to fend off the counterfeit Satan threw in his path. At the crucial moment, he saw the utter sinfulness of sin, and was able as well to see the benefits of obedience, and there was no contest. What he both escaped and gained through obedience was better by far.

Paul directed Timothy to choose the obedience option, to pursue righteousness as the necessary corollary to fleeing from everything that would enflame his youthful lusts. But he went even further. In the next chapter we'll look at what it means to pursue *faith, love and peace*. We'll also consider the importance of carrying out this pursuit arm in arm with others 'who call on the Lord from a pure heart'.

CHAPTER 8

Growing a faith that shields: Part 2

PAUL'S apostolic command in 2 Timothy 2:22, we saw, contains three pointers that can direct our minds down the right road as you and I face the challenges and temptations of a broken world every day: *'Flee … pursue … with …*

> 'Now flee youthful lusts and pursue righteousness, faith, love, and peace with those who call on the Lord from a pure heart.'

Pursuing faith, love and peace

In the previous chapter we saw that, while *fleeing* is necessary, it simply isn't sufficient. The power of temptation is never broken until it is overwhelmed by something that has an even greater pull. Only an overwhelming passion for righteousness can pull the power plug of temptation. That is why Paul commands Timothy to *pursue* it, as we saw. But Paul doesn't stop there. He goes on to include *faith, love, and peace* as worthy of diligent pursuit.

The pursuit of faith

What does it mean to pursue faith? We've already seen that *first faith* is a gift of God to us (Eph. 2:8). And we've also come to understand experientially that what we need so desperately in our battle against our sinful desires is *firm faith.* In fact, that is what this whole book is about: growing firm faith. The pursuit of faith is just that: an intentional seeking after those things that will grow the depth and vibrancy of our faith.

The pursuit of faith is simply the consistent desire to deepen your conviction that what God has for you through obedience is better by far than anything Satan and this world offer you through selfishness and sin. It is the pursuit of a stronger faith, a more knowledgeable faith, a more consistent faith, a more mature and fruitful faith. It is the daily recognition that Satan is sneaky, and that he wants to undo us all and lead us down the road of sinful pleasure, with all of its regrets and scars. It is the decision not to let him win, coupled with the understanding that to meet his challenges, you and I have to become more and more convinced that obeying God is always our very best option. We simply have to keep growing our faith.

To pursue faith is to make serious connections between what we learn about God and His ways and the challenges and opportunities we face everyday. It is understanding that those challenges and opportunities may become greater in the days ahead, and that it will take greater conviction, greater understanding and greater strength to see through sin's façade and choose the road of obedience. Simply put, the pursuit of faith is a radical determination to have a greater passion for righteousness next year than you do now, coupled with a refusal to let anything start to erode that passion.

Paul the apostle was a man who was consumed with the pursuit of a stronger, more dynamic faith. From the day he encountered the risen Christ on the road to Damascus, Paul was consistent in his belief that he needed to grow more and more in his knowledge of Christ and in the convictions that knowledge necessarily demanded. Paul never settled into a comfortable Christianity. Even though he was used by God to start several churches, bring about revival in the Gentile world, and write a majority of the New Testament epistles, Paul always considered that he needed to grow, to deepen his understanding and to pursue a more consistent, conviction-based faith.

In what is one of the more surprising verses in the New Testament, this great apostle, preacher, teacher, and writer was still pursuing his one great desire, even as he languished in prison near the end of his amazing public ministry:

> … that I may know Him and the power of His resurrection and the fellowship of His sufferings, being conformed to His death; in order that I may attain to the resurrection from the dead. Not that I have already obtained it or have already become perfect, but I press on so that I may lay hold of that for which also I was laid hold of by Christ Jesus. (Phil. 3:10-12)

Paul never stopped his pursuit of faith simply because he was desperate to 'lay hold of that for which also [he] was laid hold of by Christ Jesus'.

Like Paul, each Christ-follower has been chosen by Christ to accomplish a unique set of life objectives, to bloom where they're planted and to overcome Satan's challenges in their world, as a testimony to the power of God's rescuing hand in their lives. It will take a daily decision to pursue a stronger and more resilient faith.

The pursuit of love and peace

Let's come back to 2 Timothy 2:22 and Paul's directives to Timothy. To the pursuit of righteousness and faith, Paul now adds the pursuit of love and peace.

It is often the case that when Paul gives a list of words, he does it in some sort of order. And while we could debate whether this is the case in 2 Timothy 2:22, just think about this: the pursuit of righteousness, as I've presented it, is the key component in building a firm faith. This firm faith prefers righteousness over sin and, as a result, produces a life that acts in obedience. Just how might this obedience be characterized? Maybe as a life that overflows with authentic love, while diligent to pursue peace.

If we take just a brief look at the context of Paul's second letter to Timothy, we'll see that the church in Ephesus was facing some serious challenges and, apparently, Timothy wasn't handling things that well. Paul had to warn him against his timid stance (1:7) and encourage him to rekindle the fire of pastoral office and authority that had been his at first (1:6). Further, Timothy's challenge seems to have been that some strong men were spreading spiritually-rotten teaching and it was bringing decay to the congregation (2:16-18). It is against these twin challenges – personal weakness, and professional opposition – that Paul instructs Timothy to stand firm by pursuing righteousness, faith, love and peace. It seems reasonable that the first two – the pursuit of righteousness and faith – deal with Timothy's need for spiritual courage, while the last two – love and peace – dictate just how he is to deal with the false teachers and their dangerous doctrines. The instructions in 2:24-26, that Timothy is not to be quarrelsome, but to correct with gentleness, seem to reinforce Paul's point: A firm faith, built on the intentional pursuit of righteousness and the convictions that flow from it, frees the soul to act as Jesus acted, characterized by love, in pursuit of peace.

Let's look at Timothy's situation closely. He was being confronted with some pretty dangerous false teachers. Their 'worldly and empty chatter' (2:16-18) was described as spiritual 'gangrene' by Paul. As the spiritual guardian of the flock, Timothy was required to deal with these men, confronting their error.

He stood looking down two roads. The road of disobedience actually offered two bad choices: he could timidly refuse to deal with them, or he could tenaciously beat them up with angry words. Apparently, Timothy chose the first, since it fit best with his own personality and his selfish desires to avoid conflict. This decision brought about Paul's exhortations to be strong (2:1-6) and to solemnly instruct these men to stop their wrangling and divisive speculations (2:14, 23). Then Paul directed Timothy to choose the road of obedience, which he characterized as confronting and correcting the false teachers with gentleness, patience and kindness in the hope that God might just grant them repentance and rescue them from their captivity to Satan (2:24-26).

But how in the world could a timid man obey the call to confront with gentleness and patience? Paul is clear: 'pursue righteousness [and] faith'. Out of a firm faith will come the conviction that you can be both courageous and compassionate; you can rest in the fact that God alone will change their hearts, and you need not resort to anger or inflammatory language. Timothy, you are free to confront error passionately, out of love not hate, and to pursue peace, resting in the knowledge that God is sovereign over the affairs of His church and all things. Timothy, you are free to act in obedience and leave the results to God!

What freedom this must have given Timothy. The obedience option allowed him to pursue righteousness, escape the regret of disobedience, and all the while rest in the certain knowledge that God would always do what was best and right. He was free to choose the joy of obedience.

The same is true today. The pursuit of righteousness will grow a firm and consistent faith that will allow you and I to live out the love of Christ, and pursue peace. We can choose the obedience option and leave behind the anxiety that comes from thinking we have to orchestrate and manipulate our own success and wellbeing. The more we are convinced about God's sovereign rule over us, His lavish love for us, and His inerrant truth given to us in His Word, the more we will rest in the privilege of doing what He asks of us. Down the road of obedience, we will encounter the only joy that satisfies.

'With those ...'

So far we've looked at two pointers: 'flee ... pursue ...'. If you stopped reading right now, you might get the impression that this life of faith is a solo, that you're on your own against the brokenness of this world. Fortunately, that's not the case. But unfortunately, many Christ-followers act as though it is.

Our strategy to stand firm in righteousness – to choose the road of obedience, to be 'believing believers' with firm faith – calls us to *flee* from everything that would enflame our lustful desires. We must say 'no' to the desires of the flesh. But as necessary as it is to run from temptation, it is even more important to *pursue* righteousness, faith, love, and peace. We must consistently say 'yes' to the desires of the Spirit. Yet, there is one more component. We need to do both of these in community with other Christ-followers. Paul directs Timothy to flee and pursue 'with those who call on the Lord from a pure heart'.

As a pastor, Timothy probably felt very alone in his battles. Maybe he felt like no one understood the pressures and the challenges he faced in Ephesus. If so, he wasn't any different from you and me. It always surprises me that we all think we're in this alone. Satan does a good job of making us think that the sins we've made room for in our lives, and the temptations that continue to haunt and hunt us, are unique to us. We all think that everyone else is probably doing better than we are, and that they would stop thinking of us so well if they really knew what we were doing and what we were hiding. To top it off, we seldom if ever look at each other as allies in the fight against sin. Embarrassment keeps us quiet, and our silence keeps us alone. And Satan just keeps on smiling.

If we just stop and think, however, we'll realize a very important biblical truth that underlies Paul's directive to Timothy: the principle of *multiplied strength*. Solomon understood this, as has everyone who has ever used a rope: 'And if one can overpower him who is alone, two can resist him. A cord of three strands is not quickly torn apart' (Eccles. 4:12).

Every kid growing up knows that if trouble comes looking, it's better to be with friends. At some point, we've all learned just why the strongest rope is made up of hundreds of tiny strands wound and woven together. It's simple: the addition of strands multiplies strength.

When Paul wrote his letter, he knew the pressures and temptations Timothy would face in Ephesus. He also knew that for Timothy to *stand up* to the challenges, he had to *stand with* those who were passionate about fleeing sin and pursuing righteousness. The consistent pursuit of the obedience option demands that we give up the idea that following Christ is a solo sport. Satan just loves to find the disconnected, isolated Christ-follower who naively believes that travelling alone poses no risk. Like a lion, he is prowling around, looking to take advantage of our weaknesses. Don't venture into the jungle alone. Make it a primary focus of your Christ-following to link up with others whose hearts are pure and whose passions are driven by the delights of loving and obeying Christ. Together you'll be better able to resist that lion and send him fleeing.

So what keeps us from pursuing righteousness, faith, love and peace 'with those' who share our passion for Christ? It's simple: our pride. Somehow we think it is more noble, more praise-worthy to walk alone. We even buy the lie that spiritual strength means not needing anyone else. Once again we are called upon to make a faith-fuelled choice. If God calls us to partner with others in following Jesus, do we really think that going solo is better? Do we really believe that what the Lord asks of us is inferior to our own pride-driven agenda?

In the post-modern soup of today's society many are coming to believe that following Christ is really a personal thing; a one-on-one relationship with Jesus, specially designed and unique to the individual. The life of faith is more and more described in purely vertical terms, with little regard for the fact that each believer is not only united by faith with Christ, but is also united in faith with all those united by faith with Christ! While there certainly are benefits – eternal ones – for you and me and every individual who follows Christ, the truth is that Christianity has never come in a single-serving package.

To be a Christ-follower is to be brought into a family, to be a part of a body, to be one brick in a huge wall, and to be a member of a household (you can read it for yourself in 1 Cor. 12:14-27; Eph. 2:19; 1 Pet. 2:5; and 1 John 3:1-2). Jesus never rescued you to be alone or on your own. He took you out of trouble and put you into a group of similarly rescued folks who *together* form the dwelling He now inhabits and through whom He shines the grace and glory of the Gospel out into a broken world. The idea of the self-sufficient, independent, self-sustaining Christ-follower isn't just a myth; it's a tragic façade that Satan uses to lull us into thinking that what he offers is better than God's obedience option. It just isn't so!

So where are we?

Since you started reading this book, we've come quite a way together. We've seen that sin is really a choice, and that sinful choices stem from our inability to see obedience as the smart choice. As believers, we still act in unbelief. Our faith, though real, is weak and we are too easily overwhelmed by Satan's lies and short-lived pleasures. But it doesn't have to be this way. Faith can be strengthened, and strong faith can be the shield that extinguishes the fiery arrows of temptation. Such an 'extinguishing faith' grows out of an overwhelming passion for righteousness. This righteousness will have the effect of sharpening our spiritual vision, allowing us to see the world much more as it really is. The grand effect will be a growing recognition that God really is right in what He asks of us, and that obedience is always our very best option.

But I really need to stop right here and address something that you may be feeling. It's possible that all this talk about fleeing and pursuing and partnering has got you thinking that strong faith will be the product of your hard work. If you're the competitive sort, you're probably excited about a new challenge; if you're not, you might just be hearing the same distant sounds of failure that ran you down last time someone forced you onto the performance treadmill. Either way, please stop. The slogan, 'If it's to be, it's up to me,' might make for a catchy bumper sticker, but it's horrible theology.

While our Lord commands us to run the race set before us with endurance, the fact is that we'll never make progress on the basis of our own strength. In the next chapter we'll address this in a straightforward way. But for now, chew on this: Run the race as though the outcome depends solely upon you, and all the while rest in the knowledge that your diligence is only the sign that His strength is working mightily in and through you. Confused? Keep reading!

CHAPTER 9

Growing faith through the Spirit and the Word

TOO often as Christ-followers we find ourselves riding the pendulum as it swings back and forth between the call to spiritual diligence and the command to rest fully in Christ. Can you remember times when, after a particularly powerful sermon or seminar, you re-committed yourself to work harder at praying, reading, sharing and serving? Maybe you set out on a rigorous prayer and Bible-reading programme, and you started feeling really good about yourself after seventeen straight days of meeting and exceeding your goals. In fact, maybe you started feeling too good. Suddenly you were staring self-righteousness in the face, and it sure looked like you.

Running or resting?

At that point, all that you had heard about the sufficiency of Christ came flooding back into your thinking. Wasn't it Christ's righteousness and His strength, His power, and His forgiveness that formed the basis for your acceptance and spiritual progress before the face of almighty God? Wasn't it true that it wasn't your work but God's workmanship that made all the difference? And at that point, you began to wonder again about how they fit together: working and trusting, running and resting, your effort and Christ's finished work.

Fortunately, that question must have troubled apostle Paul, too. In several of his writings, he tackled the subject of how we are to pursue righteousness without falling into self-righteousness; how we are to run the race of faith while still resting fully in the Saviour through whom we are already counted as complete. Since I know you're anxious to know the answer, I'll give it to you in simple form and then we'll look at three places where Paul speaks directly to the issue.

> The power of God will be most evident in us when we are most diligent in the pursuit of righteousness. When we work, we know He is working. When we pursue righteousness righteously it is evidence that, through Him, we are resting fully in Him. In more personal terms, my diligence is the fruit of God's ongoing work *in* me; my humility is my response to Christ's finished work *for* me.

Studying with Paul

Have you ever thought about the fact that when we read and study God's Word it is like studying with those chosen by God to write it down? Imagine walking into your favourite coffee shop one day and seeing Paul hunched over a pile of books, furiously writing. He looks up and says, 'Hey, great to see you! If you've got a minute, I'd love to run something by you. I've been wrestling with just how my daily effort to grow in faith and the knowledge of Jesus Christ meshes with the fact that as far as God is concerned, I'm already fully accepted by Him because of what Christ has accomplished for me.' Whoa!

I know, that's a bit weird, but in some ways it is true. When we open Paul's writings, we're hearing his voice as he repeats what God Himself taught him about the very things we have questions about today. Let's listen.

Truth #1: Your diligent effort in pursuing righteousness is a good thing

Paul had lots to say to the Corinthian church, and not all of it was positive. They definitely had some problems and Paul spent years helping them find health and righteousness as individuals and as a congregation. Apparently they had some serious misunderstandings about the resurrection of Jesus and about the idea that dead people can be raised back to life. In 1 Corinthians 15 Paul gives his magnificent description and defence of this important doctrine. At the end – in verse 58 – Paul adds a 'therefore': 'Therefore, my beloved brethren, be steadfast, immovable, always abounding in the work of the Lord, knowing that your toil is not in vain in the Lord.'

Paul's final comment about the resurrection of Christ is that it is the reason we should be diligent to pursue righteousness in this life. The assurance of resurrection to life eternal some day makes the obedience option the best choice today. He makes the important point that our obedience, our effort, our work, our steadfast and strenuous pursuit of those things that constitute the 'work of the Lord', will never be for nothing. Any thought that resting in the finished work of Christ for us allows for couch-potato Christianity will find no support from Paul. Just the opposite is true. We are to press forward in the knowledge that the final victory has already been won.

Is Paul just arguing for a faith that is driven by human effort? No. At the end of the verse he puts in a very important comment: '… knowing that your toil is not in vain in the Lord'. Being 'in the Lord' is somehow vitally connected with our toil. Apparently, the Corinthians already understood the connection because Paul doesn't go on here to explain it. But fortunately, the congregations in both Philippi and Colossae needed explanations, and we get the benefit of Paul's writing to them.

Truth #2: Your diligent pursuit of righteousness is the fruit of God's work in you

The church in Philippi was one of the healthier churches described in the New Testament. Paul's letter to these Christ-followers is really fun and full of joy, as he deals not so much with problems, but with their progress in loving and following Christ. In Philippians 2:12,13 Paul hits the issue that concerns us here:

> So then, my beloved, just as you have always obeyed, not as in my presence only, but now much more in my absence, work out your salvation with fear and trembling; for it is God who is at work in you, both to will and to work for His good pleasure …

Here Paul puts it all together. First, he commands that the Philippian Christians work hard in the area of salvation. He calls them to the obedience option, with diligence pursuing Christian virtue, character and maturity. No convenient, drive-thru Christianity here. They are to 'work out [their] salvation with fear and trembling'.

Paul has made it clear in all of his other writings that the idea here is *not* that the Philippians need to work to gain salvation. Their rescue from the bondage of sin and Satan was never a cooperative operation between them and God. It was always the work of God alone, a demonstration of His undeserved and unearned grace. It had to be so because no human currency is accepted in heaven. The cash of human merit, goodness and accomplishment has no saving value in the presence of God.

Here, Paul is urging the Philippians to work hard in their pursuit of righteousness, as those who are already rescued and reformed by the power of God. They are to take it seriously because the call to walk obediently before the Almighty is a serious one. The enemy of the soul – Satan himself – is a serious enemy. The war in which they are participating cannot be fought with a casual attitude. There is a place for fear and trembling, even as they courageously march forward. Paul is calling them to recognize that the obedience option will demand their very best efforts, increasingly and consistently.

Then Paul hits the nail we've been trying to pound. He ties their diligent effort to the presence of God in their lives. He says in effect, 'God is working in you, and the result of His work is that you are willing to work hard for His glory.' This is really amazing and we won't find a more blatant demonstration of the relationship between God's work and ours. Paul doesn't try to answer all of our questions, and he doesn't pause in his letter to describe or defend further the explosive concept he's presenting. He refuses to shave the edges off either our part or God's. We're to work hard and all along understand that our work is actually the fruit of God's work in us.

I know what you may be thinking: 'If God is the one who works so that I have the will to work, and if my effort is actually the fruit of His work, then is it okay to say that when I don't feel like it, it's because God stopped working? Can I excuse my occasional spiritual laziness as His fault?' Once again, Paul comes to our rescue and speaks to us from his own experience.

Truth #3: The evidence that God is working in you is the effort expended by you in pursuit of righteousness

When he wrote to the Christ-followers in Colossae, Paul apparently was responding to some strange religious ideas that had taken root in their city. Those who were teaching some of the philosophical tenets of what later came to be known as Gnosticism were bringing confusion. At issue was the relationship between the material and the spiritual, the human and the divine, especially as it related to Jesus, the God-man. Paul was both clear and courageous in his defence of both the deity and humanity of Jesus Christ and also in his declaration that every Christ-follower was actually living in union with Christ. He put it simply: 'Christ in you [is] the hope of glory, and that's why I proclaim Him, focusing my ministry on the task of bringing others to completion in Jesus Christ!' (Col. 1:27-28, my paraphrase). In the following verse (29), Paul makes it personal, and addresses the very issue we're studying: 'For this purpose also I labour, striving according to His power, which mightily works within me.'

Paul recognized that the most important thing he could do with his life was to bring the good news of Jesus to the world. The Colossians needed to know that they could have a real, experiential, and eternal relationship with God through the Lord Jesus Christ. Paul's pursuit of righteousness in the mission of Christ through the church to the world is legendary. For this reason, it is vital that we understand his motivation and just how he understood the connection between the power of Christ *in* him, and the effort expended *by* him.

Once again, as in Philippians 2:12-13 Paul mixes two things: human effort and divine power. But here Paul sets them in a relationship that is much more than cause and effect. He doesn't describe them in a sequence or as elements in a formula. Rather for Paul, the power of God in him is really only experienced as he labours and strives to accomplish the mission God has placed before him. If we were able to ask Paul four questions, he would probably answer in ways that would help us understand his point more clearly:

- *Paul, how do you take on the day?* I labour, striving to pursue righteousness and the mission God has given me.

- *How do you labour and strive?* I labour and strive with complete dependence upon the power of God in me.

- *How do you know that God's power is working in you?* I recognize that the power of God is working mightily in me when I am striving diligently to pursue His mission.

- *Can you sum it all up?* The greatest indication of God's power in me is the effort expended by me in pursuit of His righteousness in humble dependence on Him.

> My diligence is the fruit of God's ongoing work *in me*; my humility is my response to Christ's finished work *for me*.

Growing faith

The obedience option calls every Christ-follower to diligence. Yet, too many times this call is encased in the language of sacrifice and obligation. It's what Christ-followers *have* to do, and more and more we come to view it like children forced to eat their veggies. 'Yes, they taste bad, but they're good for you!'

But if the rewards of the obedience option really are *better by far*, shouldn't we begin to understand that what God asks of us is really a privilege? Isn't the call to diligence much more of an opportunity than an obligation? I think so! If we keep in mind that as Christ-followers, all that God has for us through obedience is better by far than anything disobedience offers us, it changes our motivation. The diligent pursuit of Christian virtue, character and maturity becomes much more like Christmas morning, as we are invited by our heavenly Father to unwrap and enjoy all the gifts He has so lovingly prepared for us, His children. He has given us His Spirit and His Word, His people and His mission, His love and His ever-attentive ear. If we are truly His children, we will prize these in a way that excites our hearts and energizes our wills to know His truth, prize His ways, pursue His mission, and determine to put no restrictions on what He may ask of us as we choose the obedience option.

We must always remember that the obedience that God asks of us will also resonate with who we truly are. As new creations, our new hearts come pre-loaded with new desires that are aligned with the will of God. And while these desires will often conflict with the remaining desires of the flesh, they will always come backed up by the power of the indwelling Spirit, through whom our obedience is made possible. As we pursue these desires, diligently working to demonstrate them in our thinking and living, we will find the delight that God has attached to them.

The subject of our diligent pursuit of God – often referred to as 'spiritual discipline' – has been wonderfully studied and explained by better men than I, and so I will direct you to their work (see, for example, *Spiritual Disciplines for the Christ Life* by Donald Whitney[1]). But let me give you some foundational thoughts on the subject before we move on to the next part of the obedience option. As we have seen, our diligence in pursuing God is the evidence that God is working in us. His work is accomplished through God the Spirit, who takes up residence in the life of every Christ-follower. Our chief task is to give the Spirit free reign in our lives by eliminating the restrictive power of sin and selfishness through an increasing passion for righteousness. In this way, the obedience option grants us the privilege of increasingly being filled and fuelled by God Himself.

The Spirit: God with us

I can still remember when it really hit me that God the Spirit was living in me. I was studying the whole area of sexual immorality, and trying to put together the apostle Paul's reasons why these temptations ought to be seen as dangerous rather than exciting. There I was, knee deep in the text of 1 Corinthians 6:18-19 when Paul reached out from history and punched me in the nose:

---

1. Donald Whitney, *Spiritual Disciplines for the Christ Life* (NavPress, 1997).

Flee immorality. Every other sin that a man commits is outside the body, but the immoral man sins against his own body. Or do you not know that your body is a temple of the Holy Spirit who is in you, whom you have from God, and that you are not your own?

Paul is saying, in effect, 'Man, don't you realize that God is living in you, and that when you pursue sinful sexual practices, He's right there? Not only is He seeing it all up close and personal, but you're dragging Him into places and situations you'd never take your parents or anyone else you loved and respected!'

For the first time, I realized the magnitude of what it means to have God the Spirit as a roommate, as a resident in the house of my heart. He has come in, and He has come for a purpose. He has come to progressively transform me from a man delighted by the façade of sin, into a man who clearly sees that what God offers is truly better by far.

So what does that mean for my diligence to pursue God and His righteousness? We've already dismissed the idea that we can just sit back and let the Spirit do it apart from our diligence. But what does our diligence look like, in view of the fact that God the Spirit is an active resident in our lives? Again, I really want to point you to several books that take this whole subject much further and deeper, but here I only want to offer one thought:

> Since God the Spirit is in my life to make me more and more like Jesus, and since becoming more and more like Jesus is the very best thing I can imagine, then it only makes sense that I would do everything I can to enhance, rather than obstruct, the Spirit's work in me.

Here's an illustration that works for me, and I hope it helps you. In my yard I am fortunate to have an automatic sprinkler system. It operates on timers that open and shut valves, allowing water to flow through a series of underground plastic pipes to pop-up sprinklers and drip systems that keep our yard and potted plants well-watered all year round. It works very well unless I do something to mess it up.

Several years ago I decided to put up a full size soccer goal in our backyard. To anchor it, I drove some rather large metal spikes into the ground, not realizing that doing so pierced a series of sprinkler pipes. The next day I found water bubbling up at all four spots where the spikes had been hammered into the ground.

Trying to be that handy husband, I decided I could repair the fractures. How hard could it be? The guy at the hardware store sent me home with the right supplies and a set of instructions. I dug out around the broken pipes, cut away the broken pieces, and replaced those sections with new pieces, carefully applying primer and glue. After the specified drying time, I turned the water back on. And nothing happened. No leaks, but no sprinklers either! Later, back at the hardware store, the expert asked, 'So, did you take off the sprinkler heads so the mud could get blown out of the broken lines?' 'Nope.' I went home and did as instructed, and we had properly working sprinklers again. I was embarrassed, but I learned a great lesson. Mud in the lines keeps the water from flowing as it is supposed to! It wasn't enough to have good pipe. I also had to keep the mud from obstructing the water flow.

While there are many more things to know about how the Spirit works in our lives, this is the foundational one. As a Christ-follower, one of my primary tasks is to keep the mud of sin in all of its forms – attitudes, actions, and thoughts – from restricting the presence and power of the Spirit as He flows in my life.

This is what Solomon tells us in Proverbs 4:23: 'Watch over your heart with all diligence, for from it flow the springs of life.' Your heart and mine are the springs from which our lives flow. In Solomon's day, the spring was essential to everyday living. If its water got polluted, you were in big trouble. So they built protective walls or coverings to keep animals or other pollutants from finding their way down into the well. In the same way, sin can pollute the heart, fouling its purity, obstructing its flow. So watch over your heart diligently, keeping the pollutants of sin and selfishness away. The rewards of pure, free-flowing water are better by far.

Our role: diligence

The intentional pursuit of righteousness, faith, love, and peace calls us to a consistent exercise of the various spiritual disciplines. There are many good books on the subject, but here are some things I've found helpful in seeing the disciplines as opportunities and not just obligations.

Loving God's Word

There is no substitute for knowing God's Word, the Bible. But how you approach it makes all the difference. The Bible is not a rule book, although it does have rules in it; it isn't an encyclopedia of answer either, although there are plenty of answers in it. The Bible is an amazing story told, over thousands of years in different lands and cultures, by several storytellers, who all have been given their piece of the story by God Himself. You can't read it like you read the newspaper. You've got to read it for what it is: God's story told through the ages about His promise to re-claim and reform all that sin has polluted. At the centre of the story is the Saviour, Jesus Christ.

Here I'm going to shock you. I don't think the average Christian knows how to read the Bible, and that might just include you. Here's why.

For most of history, people did not have their own copy of the Bible. They learned the Bible and how it was to be understood as preachers taught it to them. The preachers learned to set the Bible's teaching in its historical setting and to derive eternal principles that applied to them in their world as men appointed by God. As His spokesmen they carefully and thoroughly explained the biblical text as the original writers and readers understood it. It has always been God's plan that the preaching of the Word would inform and prescribe the way individual believers understood and applied the Bible.

Today, such preaching is hard to find. Most often preachers read a text and then apply it to our day without much thought of how the original writer and readers understood it. This has led to the practice of reading the Bible as though it were written yesterday, in our world, supposedly in full sight of life as it is today. But when we open it, hoping to find something to help us with the day's challenges, the Bible often seems out of touch, its writers seeming oblivious to the way things really are. The result is that we are often disappointed with the Bible; it seems irrelevant at best, and outdated at worst. It is easily dismissed as archaic, out of touch, and even dangerous to our modern way of seeing life. Like veggies, it tastes bad, but since it is supposed to be good for us, we just keep reading it, with glazed over eyes and hearts, hoping that God will reward our faithfulness even as we secretly think the Bible is overrated.

But it isn't the Bible's fault. We need to understand it in the way God intends us to understand it. Again, there are several great books that can help you do this. More importantly, you should seek and find a church where the Bible is preached *as it was written*; that is, where the preacher opens the text and carefully explains what God was saying to the original readers, clarifying the historical and societal nuances, and extracting the eternal truth principles that God intended us all to know, applying them to our day in ways that are faithful to Him. As you sit under this kind of biblical preaching, you'll find that your personal Bible intake will become more and more exciting and helpful. You'll find it a privilege to study God and His ways at the feet of those men chosen by Him to write the Scriptures.

Having God's ear
As I listen to the wants and wishes of people around me, one of the most prominent is this: 'I just wish I had someone who would

let me be me, who I could really talk to, who would listen and be there for me no matter what.' The good news is that the almighty God has granted this deeply-felt heart wish to all who, through the indwelling Spirit, are invited into His very presence through prayer.

But as with Bible reading, prayer has really got muddled in our day. If we're honest, we have to admit that most of our praying is self-centred. Even when we start off extolling God and His greatness, it most often is just a show of praise in hopes that God will think good things of us and grant us all of our wants and needs. It's almost like we need to let God know the day's announcements and agenda so He can make sure our day goes well. We treat prayer as though it were a fax machine to heaven that puts our list of needs on God's desk so He can serve us better. No wonder prayer so often becomes a task rather than a treat. We desperately need to recover the delight that God intends His people to find. We must rediscover prayer as a singular privilege.

Understand that I am not devaluing the fact that our Heavenly Father asks us to come bearing our requests before Him. Like the best fathers, He delights to know that we need Him, and our wants and needs are a constant reminder that we are desperately dependent upon Him. Or at least they should be! And that's really my point. Prayer is a humbling event, a practice whereby our hearts are re-aligned according to the truth that God is sovereign, all-powerful, and always right. His ways are always best, and while we come to Him expressing our desires, the real privilege of prayer is that, through our submission, He moulds our desires into His. As the old slogan goes, 'Prayer changes things.' But primarily, it is God changing us, bringing our agendas and hearts into alignment with His.

Understanding that His ways are always best and right is foundational to believing that the obedience option is better by far. Even though prayer humbles us, it is in that humble dependence that we come to know the greatest freedom. We are freed from the tyranny of having to make our own way, to provide for our own wellbeing, or to orchestrate the events of the coming day, week, month and year. We can either worry and scheme, and worry some more, or we can dive into the water of trust that surrounds God's throne. Prayer gives us that opportunity.

Loving God's people

A proper reading of God's story in the Bible makes it clear that loving God the Father and following God the Son through the power of God the Spirit is not a solo adventure. Even God Himself, though One, is in community as the Three-in-One. There is simply no way to grow a faith that obeys and alone overwhelms the power of sin. God knew what He was doing when He determined that individual God-followers would dwell together in the bonds of mission and fellowship. Today it is the church. You and I are seriously misinformed if we think we can live out the obedience option without a settled determination to be a working, growing, invested part of the body of Christ, the church. These are the 'with those' with whom we are to be fleeing sin and pursuing righteousness (2 Tim. 2:22).

The post-modern idea that the church no longer has a role to play is just that, a post-modern idea. It certainly isn't a biblical idea. It is no exaggeration to say that the church today remains the *primary* way through which Jesus Christ, our risen Lord, continues to effect His mission as prophet, priest and king. It is through the preaching of the Word by those ordained through the church to gospel ministry that the prophetic voice of Christ continues to resound in our world.

It is through the ministry of baptism and the Lord's Supper that the finished work of Christ our Sacrifice is consistently extolled and courageously proclaimed as the only basis for our acceptance before Christ. These corporate privileges – granted by Christ to the church – are a constant reminder that salvation is not for the individual alone, but for a group of people that no man can number, called out of the domain of darkness and into the light of glorious union with Christ. As we partake of the Supper, we realize that we are not only united by faith with Christ, but we are also united in faith with all those so joined to Christ. The unity of the body of Christ becomes the great evidence of God's redemptive mission before a watching world.

Lastly, it is through the godly leadership of the church – men both drafted and crafted – that Christ continues to exert His kingly rule over His people. While it would be tragically wrong to assert that outside of the rule of the church there is no salvation, it would also be the essence of pride to think that you could follow Christ closely and walk the road of obedience apart from loving Christ's body – His family – the church.

In closing this chapter, I hope you sense my heart. The tension between running and resting is real and will always present a serious challenge. But take the challenge! Run with endurance, passionately pursuing a great faith, a strong faith, a faith that can overwhelm the pull of sin and its temptations. Run that race with a full reliance on Jesus Christ, knowing that your diligence is the best indication that His power is working mightily in you, as you pursue the obedience option.

CHAPTER TEN

'So what?' Putting the obedience option to the test

E ARLY in my preaching ministry I had some friends who helped me understand that 'telling' doesn't always produce 'understanding'. Lectures only produce learning if the person hearing can grasp the significance of the material. The best teachers know this and move from material to meaning, from 'here's what' to 'so what?', often. My friends helped me understand this by raising cardboard signs in the back that said 'so what?' as I reached the end of my sermons. Thanks guys!

So here's the 'so what?' of the obedience option. It can work for you. If you are truly a Christ-follower then the Spirit of God is living in you, empowering you to obey. Regardless of how you feel or where you are, the fact remains that obeying God is always your very best option. All He has for you through obedience really is better by far than anything sin and selfishness might be dangling before your eyes.

Jesus put it this way in Matthew 5:6: 'Blessed are those who hunger and thirst for righteousness, for they shall be satisfied.' Did you get that? That's God's promise to *everyone* that truly wants to be righteous, walk in righteousness and pursue righteousness through obedience to God. If you want it, you can have it.

Now I know what you're thinking. 'But I do want to be righteous but somehow sin keeps getting in the way!' As we've already seen, the truth is that we sin because we want to and we want to because we are blinded into believing that sin offers a more satisfying way to live. As we've seen, this is just Satan's deception, his façade. We've also seen that the only way to see through this façade is through the eyes of an overwhelming faith – a faith that comes to understand the much better things offered us in the pursuit of righteousness. Lastly, we come to recognize that the power of God unto righteousness will best be seen and experienced as we are diligent to pursue the obedience option. Now I want to take this strategy and show you how to put it to work in your own life. Here's the *So What*.

The race of faith

As we've seen, the overall strategy for the obedience option makes helpful use of 2 Timothy 2:22: 'Now flee from youthful lusts and pursue righteousness, faith, love and peace, with those who call on the Lord from a pure heart.' This three-part focus of *fleeing, pursuing,* and *partnership* ('with those') can keep you on track if you'll be diligent and consistent in wrapping your life around it.

But, I want to give you another word-picture for practical use, and it is found in Hebrews 12:1-3:

> Therefore, since we have so great a cloud of witnesses surrounding us, let us also lay aside every encumbrance and the sin which so easily entangles us, and let us run with endurance the race that is set before us, fixing our eyes on Jesus, the author and perfecter of faith, who for the joy set before Him endured the cross, despising the shame, and has sat down at the right hand of the throne of God.

For consider Him who has endured such hostility by sinners against Himself, so that you will not grow weary and lose heart.

Here the biblical author calls us to the race of faith, likening our lives to a marathon that we have no choice but to run. Let me quickly explain this text and then we'll see how the obedience option – choosing to build an overwhelming passion for righteousness – might be applied in the lives of a Christian man and a Christian woman.

Hebrews 12:1-2 sets up a picture in the reader's mind. It is a first-century stadium whose stands are filled with white-robed spectators. On the starting line are the runners who will begin the gruelling race that will take them out of the stadium, down the worn paths of the city, out into the countryside, and then back to the stadium for a glorious finish. Some will finish strong. Others will give up and end up littered along the route.

The author intends us to see ourselves as running this race. As we stand at the starting line we look up to see the spectators, like so many white clouds. But they are more than spectators. They are those who have already finished the race and they are 'witnessing' to us that we can succeed as well.

Many of these spectators have been mentioned in the previous chapter (Heb. 11) that has often been called 'Faith's Hall of Fame'. But actually that is a confusing title. Chapter 11 of Hebrews isn't the story of extraordinary people. It is the story of what an extraordinary God has accomplished through ordinary people who chose to order their lives by faith. For them, faith was the life-dominating conviction that whatever God had for them through obedience really was *better by far* than anything they could have gained through selfishness and sin. As we stand ready to begin our race they are telling us by their presence that we too can finish the race, but only if we follow the strategy they followed. The first step is to 'lay aside every encumbrance' and the 'sin which so easily entangles us'.

In the ancient world athletes trained with large bronze bands around their biceps, thighs, and ankles. The author refers to them as 'encumbrances' and that's just what they are if they are not used properly. In training for the race, these weights stressed their muscles and made them stronger. But those things that had their place in practice were a hindrance when running the race and needed to be cast aside. The author is making an important point: some things that are profitable can become hindrances when used improperly. These 'encumbrances' can slow us down when it comes time to run the race of faith.

Likewise the 'easily-entangling sins' had to be overcome. The words here compare sin to low-lying vines that often grew across the runners path, especially out in the countryside. The fatigued runner, if not careful, could easily be tripped up by these seemingly weak little vines. To win, both the weights and the sins had to be cast away.

But even more important than saying 'no' to the weights and sins was saying 'yes' to Jesus, the one on whom the persevering runner had to focus his eyes throughout the race. To be successful the runner must not focus on his own fatigue and pain but on the one who is both the author and perfecter of the very faith that carries him on. This Jesus has already run a much more difficult race and He stands in front of the runner, inviting him to run hard even while resting in the fact of His love and power.

Each day as we follow Christ we are running the race of faith. Each day we will face myriad choices as challenges, opportunities and temptations present themselves to us. Each day we will have to say 'no' to those encumbrances and sins that weigh us down while saying 'yes' to Jesus. This is just like Paul's charge to Timothy, that he 'flee' youthful lusts, while 'pursuing' righteousness, faith, love and peace. As we've seen, there's a third part and that's to do it all with others who share our desire to follow hard after Jesus Christ.

Putting the obedience option to work

So now you know the theology and the theory behind the obedience option. But, the question that has to be asked and answered is this: how does it work in daily living? Let's attempt an answer by looking at an example of how it might work in your life, as a Christian man or Christian woman. While you might be tempted to read only the chapter that applies to you, it might just be a great benefit to read both. You never know what the Lord might do in helping you understand those in your life of the opposite sex.

CHAPTER ELEVEN

The obedience option and the Christian man

AS men we face a distinctive set of challenges in our pursuit of the obedience option. We live very complex lives made up of obligations and challenges at work and in the home. Don't forget that we were also wired by God to compete and conquer. It all adds up to make almost every day an adventure in recognizing that what God has for us through obedience is always our very best option. Every day we face the opportunity to quit running, to give in to the pull of temptation, to pursue the desires of our lusts and choose the road of disobedience. But it doesn't have to be that way. Over time, as we build our shield of faith, we can live more confidently for Christ, delighting in the obediences He calls us to and running the race that is set before us with an endurance that He both demands and enables.

Recognizing our encumbrances

As we line up to run the race we first have to take a look at the weights that we're carrying. Remember, these weights are good things that, if used improperly, become encumbrances that hinder our running.

Take a moment and think about some of the things in your life that, while profitable and helpful, often become problem areas in your race of faith. Could it be that your strict discipline on the job makes you a tyrant at home? Does your diligence and high work-rate make it difficult for you to rest and relax with your family? Or, on the other end of the spectrum, has your preoccupation with a hobby or leisure pursuit begun to strangle your relationship with your wife and kids? How about your preoccupation with money? Are you so locked into having enough that you find it hard to be generous? Or maybe you're prone to go the other direction and have taken the obligation to provide for your family too far, so now are locked in the grip of greed and debt. I could go on, but I think you get the picture. Good things, good characteristics and plans, while needed and helpful, can also become those things that hinder our obedience to Christ if they are not recognized and removed at the proper time!

While each of us has our own weights and encumbrances, there are a couple of fundamental ones that we all need to recognize and deal with righteously. God created man first, giving him the strength necessary both to work and to lead. These two essential elements of manhood – work and leadership – are both found in Genesis 2:15-25. God created Adam, and immediately 'put him into the garden of Eden to cultivate it and keep it'. Here we find the first instance of work in the human realm. In this work, Adam is asked to imitate God, the first workman (see Gen. 2:2-3). When God gave Adam a job to do, He was also giving Him a way to worship, to reflect God Himself, in the daily affairs of life.

Next, God put Adam in a position of leadership, asking him not only to manage the Garden, but also to name the animals. In the Old Testament, the naming of something signified leadership. To make the point even better, God next put Adam in a position of leadership in the first marriage, when He brought Eve into the world, as a helper for Adam.

As men God has called us to work hard and to be leaders in our families. Yet, as noble as this calling is, too often our work and our leadership style become encumbrances to us as we run the race of faith.

In our work it is essential that we keep the correct perspective. God created work so that we could mimic Him, in the creation and maintenance of that which is good and brings glory to Him. The glory of God is the goal, and the work He gives us is a means by which we can demonstrate that glory, through our diligence, excellence and righteous business practices. Yet we too often get it turned around! We make work the goal and God the means whereby our goals and dreams can be reached. Be honest. You and I too often are preoccupied with the challenges and opportunities our careers provide (or we hope they will provide at some point!) and see God as the one who can help us get what we want. Our prayers are selfish, and our focus is on the job much more than on the Lord. No wonder we stumble in our race. We've still got the weights on and our focus is in the wrong place.

As leaders God has called men to be courageous, to be out in front, aware of the challenges ahead and prepared to guide their families through them safely. Leadership demands strength, and God has graciously given us that strength, and commanded us to use it in a way that brings Him glory, that makes Him look good. But too often we use our strength selfishly, and sometimes our selfishness keeps us from using it at all. How ironic that, when it come to leadership, we men can misuse it in two very opposite ways.

Sometimes we misuse our position as leaders by refusing to be compassionate and 'others-oriented' in our leading. We'd rather just command and expect everyone to jump. While we hate that leadership style when someone applies it to us, we seem all too ready to employ it at home. At that point God's gift to us becomes a club that we use with devastating results. Of course God never meant it to be this way. He intends that we mimic His leadership. He asks us to be servant-leaders, wielding the power of our position with courageous humility, taking our job seriously but never ourselves.

On the other hand sometimes we misuse our leadership role by failing to lead at all. Over the years of pastoral ministry it has become abundantly clear to me that what most women want from their husbands, and the fathers of their children, is leadership! They want their men to have a plan, to set a direction, to guard and guide the family in the ways of God, to be champions rather than lazy chumps. They are quite tired of us being too tired, sick of us being selfish, and at their wits' end over the fact that they have to lead while at the same time training our kids to think that we're in charge. Too often we have taken the gift of leadership and turned it into an encumbrance for ourselves and our families by ducking our responsibilities. Once again we've become focused on ourselves rather than on Jesus. It's time to deal with the encumbrances, and fix our eyes on Him.

Laying aside our encumbrances

Once you've recognized the encumbrances that are holding you back, you've simply got to deal with them. Here's where the obedience option works. Think right now of one encumbrance. It might be leadership or career, money or fun. Here's the truth: What God has for you through obedience is better by far.

Let's remember just why we find ourselves with the encumbrances: It is because we have chosen to keep wearing them! It is essential to admit that, for whatever reasons, we have found a certain benefit in those things that are actually hindering us. The choice now is to recognize them no longer as benefits but as what they have become through our misuse: hindrances to our pursuit of righteousness.

Begin to understand the benefit of using your weights the right way. Take work, for example. Do you understand how your job, your career, fits into God's plan for you? Why not start your own study project, using the Bible, and some of the helpful resources your pastor or other spiritual leaders might recommend, to find out what God thinks about work. In this way, you'll be pursuing righteousness. Then, find some other men and share what you've learned. Keep at it! The rewards for your health, family, and the kingdom are tremendous, and you probably don't even know it. The same strategy can work for your leadership at home, or any number of other encumbrances you've managed to pick up over the years. Start now! Make a list of the things God asks of you, and the benefits of obedience, and you'll soon agree that what God wants is actually better by far.

Recognizing our sin

The writer of Hebrews 12 moves on from the 'encumbrances' to the 'sin which so easily entangle us'. These are the sins that we've made a place for, that we have allowed to find a home in our lives. They're our pet sins, those we have actually come to believe are not harmful. That's why they so easily entangle us, because we've stopped seeing them as a threat. Maybe it is the calculated but lustful glance that you've perfected, or even a mental fantasy that you've rationalized as being good for you. Maybe it is that excitement you feel when you buy a new watch or suit or power tool, an excitement that is slowly becoming addictive, even as the desire to get more stuff crowds out the righteous desire to be generous. As men, we have so many closets in our lives in which we can store our pet sins, away from the public eye – and yet, the care and feeding of these sins is something we choose to continue. Remember, as Christ-followers, in whom the Spirit of God has taken up residence, we don't sin because we have to; we sin because we want to! We sin because we have foolishly come to believe that sin – disobedience before God! – will actually give us what we want, bring us more pleasure and make our lives better. Of course, in our hearts we know this is a myth, and a dangerous one at that.

Let's take the big one as an example of how to deal with other sins. Of course I mean lust. Every man knows that sexual desire is a constant in his life. Add to that a world that has become expert in putting sensuality in front of men at every turn and you have a daily battle that threatens every man at the very core of his being. All around us we see men giving up, and giving in to the addictive power of sexual fantasy and pornography. We used to have to sneak it. Now it is electronically piped into our laptops and smart phones, available at the end of a few easy keystrokes. Every Christ-following man – myself so included! – deals with this every day, and he does so either from the position of faith, or unbelief.

So what do we do?

First we have to agree that what God has for us through obedience is really *better by far* than anything – including glossy pictures, and well-shot videos – that Satan can offer us through selfishness and sin. If we can't agree on this we ought to question whether the Spirit dwells in us.

Second we simply have to *flee youthful lusts!* We have to take steps to safeguard our hearts, and those of our family, from the poison of sexual temptation. I could rehearse all the don'ts, but chances are good that you already know them! Chances are also good that you've tried them and you still have never got to the place where the temptations have lost their power. You've said 'no' to the flesh – which is good! – but that alone will never diminish the pull of lust. It simply isn't enough to say 'no' to the flesh; we have to say 'yes' to the Spirit, and to the pursuit of righteousness. We have to create such a passion for righteousness that it overwhelms our passion to sin.

Dealing with our sin

Having recognized and dealt with our encumbrances, and admitted the presence and power of our pet sin of lust, we must commit to a passionate pursuit of righteousness in the areas of our sexuality, and the control of that lust. We only have two choices: run with endurance the race set before us, or give up and give in! But for the Christ-following man, the only real choice is to endure through temptation, to run hard after Christ. Anything else will be our undoing. That's where the obedience option comes into play.

As we come to understand that we sin, not because we have to, but because we want to, we also come to realize that we can strengthen our desire for righteousness so that it overshadows the desire for sin. This is a break-through concept for many men in the area of sexual temptation. As they commit themselves to finding and grasping what God's Word has to say about their sexuality, they come to see that God's ways really are better by far. They also come to understand the ruin that awaits those who indulge their appetite for unrighteous excitement. They become painfully aware of the danger that disobedience poses, even as they come to see the lasting satisfaction that stems from remaining faithful to Christ.

Let me use an example that puts it all together in the area of sexual temptation.

Let's say that the lust you and I harbour, as Christ-following men, is like a mean, powerful gorilla. He lives inside of us, and he is intent on destroying our lives. He wants to destroy our marriages, our families, our testimony as Christ-followers, our reputations – everything. He is the gorilla of lust, and we can either feed him or starve him. Feeding him feels good at the moment, but with every feeding, he grows stronger. Whether it is a few minutes with the *Sports Illustrated, Swimsuit Edition*, or an internet porn session, each time we try to satiate our lustful longings with that which is unrighteous, his power over us grows stronger, and so does his appetite. Slowly we begin to recognize that it takes more and more to satisfy him, even as we're blind to the fact that we are becoming addicted to an excitement that is unrighteous. This unrighteous excitement is Satan's counterfeit. It looks like the real thing, and even feels like the real thing at first, but in reality it is not the stuff of life. It doesn't satisfy; it kills.

As men, God wired us for sexual satisfaction. Yet it is all too easy for us to become dependent on the unrighteous excitement that springs from wicked sources. Unrighteous excitement is like drinking saltwater. At first, the cold liquid feels good, and gives the impression of satisfying your thirst, while all the time it is actually intensifying your need for pure water. It is a cause masquerading as a solution. If you don't recognize it for what it is, eventually it will kill you. The same is true of sexual lust when we try to satisfy it with the fruit of an unrighteous tree.

The gorilla of lust feeds on unrighteous excitement, demanding greater and more intense amounts. Eventually he will become the dominant power in our lives, propelling us to take greater risks, to try more desperate measures to keep him satisfied. Sadly this will most often take men across a line they never intended to cross, into fornication, or adultery, or some other form of sexual perversion that will forever alter the course of their lives. By the time they come to their senses it will be too late to escape the relational pain and death that they will have brought down upon themselves and those that love them.

But it doesn't have to be that way. What God offers down the road of obedience is better by far, and Christ-following men can build a cage of righteousness in which to capture and contain the gorilla. While I don't think we can ever kill him, we can certainly starve him and at the same time so strengthen the cage that he will be unable to break out and bring ruin to our lives.

A strong cage is just another way of describing an overwhelming passion for righteousness, a faith that shields the heart and life from sexual temptation. It also seems that there is a connection between strengthening the cage and starving the gorilla. If we feed the gorilla, it seems to weaken the cage. On the other hand, strengthening the cage seems to starve and weaken the gorilla. As we pursue righteousness, building up a passion for that which God loves, there is an inverse reaction to the power of lust. We come to see unrighteous excitement for what it really is: death, not life. Over time, it loses its urgency, its power, its hold on our hearts.

The place to start, as a Christ-follower, is with God's perspective on your sexuality. As it turns out, sex was God's idea, and He didn't think of it as dirty. In fact, He designed it for our pleasure, as a beautiful and satisfying element in our marriages. He wired us to experience great excitement sexually, but only within the bounds of marriage. It is here that our pursuit of righteousness must begin.

If you are married the 'better by far' part of the equation is all about your wife. She is God's provision for your sexual satisfaction, even as you are for her. Healthy sexuality is an essential part of marital fulfilment and joy and it is so important that, in your pursuit of righteousness in this area, you remain aware of what is at stake. Your gorilla is trying to break out of the cage and ruin your marriage, your home, your kids and your life. But if you understand God's plan, and truly believe that what He has for you is better by far, then the advances of the gorilla will be seen as just what they are: death for you!

Imagine that you're home alone. Your family is gone for several hours. Unlike your office computer that has all kinds of firewalls and porn screens, your personal laptop at home is completely unfettered and unguarded. So, since it's been a tough week, and you're feeling a bit underappreciated, you decide to surf the web and find some nice porn to infuse some excitement into your life. You've done it so many times before, and got away with it, right?

But before you wake up your PC, let's think this through. Let's hit the passion pause button and consider the obedience option. You're looking down two roads: the one takes you to porn and the other takes you to Christ. Here's how it goes:

Over the past months your times in the Word and prayer and discussions with other Christian brothers have filled your heart with some powerful truths about your heart, your susceptibility to lust and the place of your marriage in God's plan for your life. You've really opened up to these guys and to your wife and committed to run the race of faith with endurance. You're more and more aware of the privilege you have of being a child of God, and a partner with Jesus Christ in showing off His grace and glory. So, because you've come to really believe that obedience is better by far, you start through the strategic thinking plan you've put together. Here's the conversation you begin to have with yourself.

1. First admit that you really don't have to do this. You want to because there is an electricity in unrighteous excitement that both your mind and body remember. It is at this point that memory is really strong – but the strength of that memory is based on a lie. Don't you also remember how you felt last time? Haven't you been reflecting also on the fact that what seems irresistible in this moment really is not as powerful as the euphoria you'll feel if your act righteously? You know the truth: You really don't have to do this! Remember that verse in 1 Corinthians that you and the guys memorized?

> No temptation has overtaken you but such as is common to man; and God is faithful, who will not allow you to be tempted beyond what you are able, but with the temptation will provide the way of escape also, so that you will be able to endure it. (1 Cor. 10:13)

Be a man and admit that you aren't being forced to go down the road of lust. There's no gun to your head! You just want to do it. Say it: 'I want to sin!' So how does that feel? What does that say about you? Aren't you a bit concerned about what it says about your heart and your trust in Jesus Christ that you're so easily going to fill your mind with pictures that will inflame your sexuality with unrighteous excitement? You know God is seeing this, and is not happy! Your Lord Jesus is also seeing this, and despite the fact that He took all the wrath for your sins, you're still going to reap the discipline a wayward son deserves. Is this really worth it?

2. Second, you do realize, don't you, that it won't really satisfy. It never has before. It has only left you wanting what you could never have, while at the same time hardening your heart toward the wife that you do have. And she is really a wonderful, godly, gracious woman. She is God's gift to you. Are you really going to do this – sin against God and your wife? You've learned that porn will make you angry and resentful toward her and will even decrease the satisfaction you might derive from marital intimacy. It never delivers what it promises anyway. What looks like life is really death. You know it. Now believe it.

Remember how you did that study project on the beauty of a godly wife? Remember reading through Proverbs 31 and recognizing just how valuable your wife was? Remember that discussion you and the guys had about the women on the computer you're about to lust after? They're someone's sister; someone's daughter. Don't forget, that woman's sins, and yours, were the very reason your Saviour suffered and died on the cross. He did it, not so you could continue to choose the poisonous pleasures of sin, but so that He might rescue you out of darkness and futility and bring you into the very family of God. What are you thinking?

3. But there's more! Third, what about your faith in God? What about your belief that His ways are best? Has something changed? Has He been holding out on you? Are the sexual façades Satan is building in your life really going to make it better? By this time, you've hopefully come to your senses. Your

passionate pursuit of righteousness has kicked in, and you've come to see that giving in to sexual temptation is really not going to enhance life. It is really death to you, to your marriage and to your obedience to Christ. You can do better, and you do, because you know that what God has for you through obedience really is better by far. So you smack the gorilla in the mouth and lay another layer of iron on the cage. Then you spend some time in prayer thanking God for the euphoria of obedience, for the freedom of purity and for your wonderful wife, before thinking of a great way to welcome her home.

Of course, what you've just read is a greatly abbreviated version of just how the obedience option might work its way out in your life. But, the main points are there:

- You realize that your sin is a result of your own choice. You sin because you want to!

- You also understand that the only way to curb your 'want to' regarding sin is to have an overwhelming 'want to' in regard to righteousness.

- And so you run the race with endurance, building an overwhelming passion for righteousness through consistent study of God's Word, prayer, and partnership with others who share your desire for God and His ways.

- Then, when temptation hits, you no longer remain passive, but intentionally work to see it through the lens of righteousness; to recognize that it is really not life, but death; to understand the full consequences of a sinful choice and to compare it with the euphoria of obedience and its rewards.

- Over time you are much more consistent in recognizing that what God offers you through obedience really is better by far! You might even start keeping a careful record of God's gracious gifts to you and your family; and be ready always to affirm that what God demands is always your very best option.

- What you come to recognize is that the power of God in you is being displayed through your passionate pursuit of His best. That's real faith! That's a faith that endures, through the uphill portions of the race; a faith that more and more prizes the face of Jesus, as you hear Him say; 'Well done, you good and faithful follower!'[1]

---

1. See Matthew 25:21.

CHAPTER TWELVE

The obedience option and the Christian woman

FROM the beginning of this book I haven't hidden the fact that I'm a man. That means that the previous chapter was easy for me to write, because I live it every day. It is also easy for me to call other men to pursue the obedience option because I've done it – am doing it! – and guess what? It works. Though I am not perfect, and never will be this side of heaven, I no longer hide behind the lie that I am powerless in the face of sin's allure.

Writing about the challenges facing Christian women is much harder, however, for obvious reasons. Fortunately for us all, I married an incredible Christian woman whose freedom in Christ has allowed her to be honest about the areas where she and others who sincerely love and follow Christ harbour encumbrances and sins that so easily can trip them up. If this chapter has any benefit, it is due to Cherylyn's insight, honesty, and authentic passion to pursue the obedience option in her race of faith. As you read, imagine that my wife is writing from her heart to yours.

Recognizing Our Encumbrances

As women we don't have an easier race ahead of us. Following Christ – whether for a man or a woman – will mean running the same course, exerting the same effort, and displaying the same endurance. It will also demand the same strategy: saying 'no' to those things that weigh us down, and focusing our passion on Jesus, the one who can grow our faith as we pursue righteousness, faith, love, and peace with those who call upon God from a pure heart.

The only difference is that our challenges, our temptations, our encumbrances and our sins come in different packages than those that face Christian men. While we can't take the time to describe even a handful of the most prevalent, we can take a look at two of the big ones.

When it comes to encumbrances, remember that these are attitudes or activities that in their place are good, like the weights used in training. They only become encumbrances when we allow them to get out of hand, to operate out of their given place, to become masters over us instead of the servants they were meant to be.

If we're honest as women we'll admit that one of the biggest encumbrances we carry is our society's understanding of *image*. How are we to think and feel about the way we look? How does this align with God's view of us, and our physical attractiveness?

The truth is that God created us women to be attractive: in our physical make-up, our feminine allure and our ability to care and nurture, among other things. Adam – created by God and given a position of leadership over the Garden and all the animals – was so incomplete that God said it was 'not good'. Adam was alone, incomplete. God remedied the situation by bringing Eve, a helper that suited Adam. Only a blind man would argue that feminine beauty was not a big part of God's blueprint in creating a woman that would eclipse a man's devotion to himself and his work. He made Eve in such a way that Adam was drawn to her, recognized her great value and wrapped his life around her. This was, and is, God's design.

But our society has made image into an idol. We Christian women are constantly having to battle the urge to buy into this idolatry. If we're honest, we have to admit that there are very few days when we are satisfied with the way we look. If it isn't our hair, waistline, ankles or complexion, it's our crows feet, bust line, saggy arms or broken nails! So here's the deal: In its place, taking care to be at our best is a good thing, honouring to the God who made us shapely and beautiful. But, all too often we let it go too far. We worry, rant, complain, and then we spend, and spend; ultimately, after expending both energy and dollars, we realize nothing has really changed: we're still dissatisfied with our image! Sadly, we realize that the good thing God has given us – our womanly image – has become a weight so heavy that it becomes a dominant force in our lives. We become driven: not by a passion for Christ and a righteous inner beauty, but by the desire to be desirable, as our culture defines it.

Let me briefly mention another possible encumbrance. There is no question but that God has instilled in women a gift for nurturing, for caring, for helping. Perhaps the greatest display of this is in the home. Despite the fact that women can – and should – be free to use their skills and savvy as salt and light in the marketplace, it is undeniable that motherhood brings together all of the uniquely wonderful abilities and sensitivities God instilled in women.

In its place, the natural drive of a mother to care for her children is among the most righteous and beautiful things God has given to humanity. I've had three children, and watched my oldest daughter give birth to a beautiful daughter. Nothing else even comes close to the joy and satisfaction I have found in loving, shaping, training, teaching and even disciplining our children.

Yet with this tremendous privilege comes a great challenge. Too often, we moms can become so child-centred that our lives get way out of balance. We can become so child-centred that other areas of our lives suffer. Our marriages suffer as we neglect our husbands; our souls suffer as we neglect our spiritual disciplines; and our relationships suffer as we find less and less desire to be with the church and those friends with whom we ought to be pursuing righteousness, faith, love and peace, as we run the race together.

I know that there are seasons in motherhood where there simply isn't time even to shower regularly! I've been there. But let's be honest. Sometimes we find it easier to be a mom than to be a wife, a friend, a woman through whom the Spirit of God wants to shine His light. It is at that point, as we are being called by Jesus to run the race set before us with endurance, that we simply have to let go of an encumbering, distorted mothering commitment which, if we're honest, is neither good for us or for our family. Think about one more thing: at some point, you're going to have to let go of your children, and watch as they walk out the door to be on their own. Better to deal with the encumbrance now, to put your God-given devotion as a mother in the proper place, knowing that what God asks of you down the road of obedience is actually the very best for you and for your children.

Laying aside our encumbrances

As with all encumbrances the weight of image isn't easily laid aside. Let's be honest, once laid aside, we'll find that we've picked it up tomorrow. But, if we're to run the race of faith with the kind of righteous endurance that is required, we're going to have to find ways to keep image in its proper place. And the obedience option can help.

To begin, we simply have to admit the way we feel. We feel inadequate and we feel imperfect. What's more, we feel threatened by the fact that others certainly look perfect and more than adequate! We're in the image race, and we're falling further and further behind. Then we have to admit that this whole line of thinking is actually the selfish residue of our decision to look at ourselves through the wrong lens. We have chosen to buy into the world's definition of image, and we ought to be ashamed of ourselves. Our shame should stem from the fact that the Lord Jesus Christ has redeemed us for a much greater purpose than the latest fashion trend. We are His workmanship – His craftsmanship – created in Christ Jesus for the purpose of displaying His goodness and grace to a watching world. We need to rest in the fact that what God has for us through obedience to His heart and His Word really is better by far than the glamour and glitz this world is selling. He is busy restoring the only image that truly lasts. He is renewing us in the image of Christ.

Perhaps this will help. We've just got to adopt God's view of us. The Bible is quite clear that God actually does have an opinion about our physical bodies and even our appearance. Paul reminded the Christ-followers in Corinth that their bodies were actually a temple, a dwelling place of God Himself: 'Do you not know that you are a temple of God and that the Spirit of God dwells in you?' (1 Cor. 3:16).

I know it is wrong to pour too much into this verse, but I think we can all agree that it is right and good to treat our physical bodies with care. Further, as women, our femininity and physical attractiveness is a crucial part of God's design for marital intimacy. Take some time to read Song of Songs and notice the great number of times the bridegroom compliments his bride on her physical attractiveness and sexual allure. Beauty is a good thing, and every godly husband wants his godly wife to look good, smell good and be good. But even more importantly, every godly husband will appreciate more and more a godly wife whose inner righteousness radiates a beauty that eclipses that of the physical. This is the view from heaven. As Christ-followers we need to prize that view and never forget our responsibility to lay aside any pursuit of image that is selfish and idolatrous. He has not redeemed us to become examples of this world's obsession but to be samples of His freeing grace and renewing righteousness.

Dealing with the temptation to retreat from life into the world of mothering will again require an honest look into our hearts. Are we caring for our children, or are we consumed with them? Are we finding it more and more to our liking to hide behind the chores of motherhood rather than deal with the complexities of the race of faith? Simply put, have our children become our god?

Every Christian parent understands that children are God's gift to us. But it was never His intention that we become so focused on the gift that we fail in our adoration and service to the Giver. After all, in reality, these children are really His, on loan to us for a season. They are ours as His stewards, entrusted with the responsibility to live righteously before them, running the race of faith with endurance and a steadfast focus on the Saviour. They are ours as His servants, privileged to teach, love, serve, and send out these children as those who honour His Son and obey His Word. As mothers, we must never lose this focus! All of our divinely instilled mothering prowess will count for nothing if we are not equally committed to modelling a passion for Christ before our children. The encumbrance of child-centred living will not only slow us down in our race; it will seriously hinder our children as they prepare for theirs.

Recognizing our sin

Among Christian men it is easy to get agreement on enemy number one: the gorilla of lust. With Christian women, it isn't quite so easy. But, in order to walk through just how the obedience option might look in the life of a female Christ-follower, let's agree to agree on a couple of challenges most women face. After

the first set of sins brought corruption and death into our world,
God had this to say to Eve:

> To the woman He said,
> 'I will greatly multiply your pain in childbirth,
> In pain you will bring forth children;
> Yet your desire will be for your husband,
> And he will rule over you.' (Gen. 3:16)

One thing that is painfully obvious in this verse is that the
original created harmony in marriage was corrupted by sin.
Fundamental to this corruption was the fact that, while being
invested with the privilege of motherhood, women would be
caught in the tension of wanting to control their environment,
while still being asked to follow the leadership of their husband,
even though this leadership would now often be tyrannical. You
only have to look across the page from Genesis 3:16 to see that the
same word ('desire') is used by God in speaking to Cain about
the fact that sin, like an angry animal is just waiting to overpower
him (see Gen. 4:7). Sin brought something into the female world
that carries with it the temptation to control individually that
which was meant to be addressed harmoniously in marriage.

What a mess! It seems that Satan's chosen target in trying to
undermine God's creation was marriage. As strange as it may
seem, Satan must have realized that marriage played an essential part in God creation plan, and he determined to corrupt that
plan by blowing up the Creator's marital blueprint. God's design
of loving, male leadership and willing female helping and
completing was radically re-oriented through the selfishness of
sin, made attractive by Satan's subtle seductions.

As women we can understand the effects of Eve's sin in our
lives, and some of our greatest temptations flow from this. Let me
suggest a couple, and please understand if I paint with a really
broad brush. After all, I'm just trying to set out a temptation that
we can use to illustrate the obedience option.

Given our sense of nurture, it is often the case that we look after things in a different way than men do. They want achievement and success. We want our lives and homes to be places of safety. While they prize significance, we prize security for ourselves, our children and our world. Safety allows for relationships to prosper and that resonates with how we see life. But this can present two constant temptations to sin.

First, we can tend toward being overly afraid. While our God-given instincts are actually His way of making us better at being protected and protectors, it is all too easy for us to live our lives in a constant state of fear. Like a low-grade fever this fear seems always to be there, always just below the surface. It is a kind of fear that can never be fully calmed simply because it is focused on those things that can never be fully dealt with or consistently controlled. While this fear may increase our diligence and vigilance, we have to admit that it almost always threatens to erode the practical application of our faith and trust in the Lord. Our daily temptation is to understand the limits of righteous vigilance, and not give in to our desire to let the fear of the known and the unknown become a dominating force in our lives. If it does, it can push us or paralyze us. It can replace trust with trying, and displace that sense of peace and rest that Christ alone can give us in the midst of this broken world.

The second way our passion for safety and security can bring temptations to sin is through the desire to control. Again, while our drive to provide a safe place for others is good, and from God, we can easily become addicted to having everything the way we think it should be. We can begin to find our security in having things just right, according to our plan, aligned with what we have determined is best and right. While this is certainly not just a female tendency, you know that this becomes the source of our nagging on the one hand, and our constant state of discontent on the other. We push – and we purchase. Somewhere along the line, we lose that harmony and life-partnership that our passion for safety was meant to foster in the first place. We become individualized, feeling that no one else understands, and determining to get the job done our way. Then we look back and recognize that we've been seduced into imitating Eve, who determined to act alone, in control of her own destiny. And you know how that ended.

Dealing with our sin

We simply have to find ways to keep our need for safety and security from becoming vehicles for the sins of fear and control. It appears that we may have twin gorillas! But, fortunately for us, both can be confined – and controlled! – in a single cage. Like the gorilla of lust in the male world, our gorillas of fear and control must be captured and contained in a structure built out of the truth of God, and maintained through a daily pursuit of righteousness. Let's see how the obedience option might make this a reality in our lives.

Admitting our sin

Our starting place is just to be honest and admit that our sin can't be blamed on Eve, or on our situation or circumstances. We've denied or blame-shifted long enough. Let's just go before our heavenly Father and admit that we sin because we want to! There is something electric and satisfying about being in control, and even if the fear we carry is both demoralizing and distressing, it actually gives purpose to our lives, in a weird, twisted sort of way. But, it doesn't have to be this way! In fact, God never intended it to be this way. Admitting that we have some gorillas, and that they've been on the loose too long, is the first step to resisting their power and building a cage that can keep them from getting in the way of our race of faith.

Fleeing youthful lusts

As we've seen, our first call is to flee from these sinful ways of looking at and living our lives. We need to flee from those things that strengthen our gorillas. With the men, fleeing youthful lusts is easy to describe. Just stay away from those things that arouse a desire for unrighteous excitement. But what do we do? What do we flee from? The answer is: those things that excite in us an inordinate fear or improper desire to control or change. Maybe for you it is reading the newspaper with all of its emotionally-charged headlines of tragedy and panic. Maybe it is the group of ladies you drink coffee with, whose stories and gossip fuel in you a desire to have more and more in order to gain the sense of well-being that drives you. Maybe it's a hundred different sources of information, or thoughts that stick in your head, to be used later as the building blocks of ungrounded concern or an intense desire to upgrade some area of your life unnecessarily.

Pursuing righteousness

But remember, while saying 'no' to the desires of our flesh is necessary, it certainly isn't sufficient! The strength of the obedience option is not in running away, but in running to, in saying 'yes' to the desires of the Spirit. It is the pursuit of righteousness that builds within us a delight in perceiving and living life God's way. His way is always best, always right and our finest option.

If the male gorilla is caged in a structure of holiness, strengthened through righteous contentment and purity, our twin gorillas of fear and control must be kept in a strong cage fashioned out of deep rest in the sovereignty of our almighty heavenly Father. This cage will be maintained through a constant realization of, and reliance on, the truth of God, especially in the areas of faithfulness to His people and His promises of sovereign care for all eternity. The pull of inordinate fear and control will never be overcome except by those whose hearts and minds have been intoxicated with the reality of God's power and promises.

With those who call upon God

The place to start is a good understanding of the biblical story. Find some friends and start with Genesis. Watch as Moses, writing to a wandering group of discouraged Israelites, stresses the care with which God created all things, for the wellbeing of humanity. Hear how he impresses on His readers that, in spite of their precarious position in the desert, they can rely on the faithfulness of their covenant-keeping God to lead, guide, provide, and protect them if they will but trust Him! And don't stop there! Continue your adventure by following God through Exodus, as He brings His people out of bondage and into the Promised Land. Keep going through the Old Testament, hearing the prophets speak comfort and courage to the people, even in times of peril, based on God's promise to one day send the 'He' of Genesis 3:15, who would turn curse into blessing, overcoming death and sin, and announcing the re-entrance of heavenly authority into the earthly realm. I could go on and on! The point is this: only a deep understanding and steadfast trust in the sufficiency and faithfulness of our sovereign King can build that shield of faith capable of keeping the fiery darts of fear and control at bay. As your focus becomes more and more the things of God, you will find that, as the hymn 'Turn Your Eyes Upon Jesus' says, '… the things of earth will grow strangely dim/ In the light of His glory and grace'.

Putting the obedience option strategy to work

At crucial times of the day, we stand looking down the roads before us. Perhaps an event or a news item has reminded us just how unsafe this world is. Maybe it's the feeling we still have that we're vulnerable, even after checking every door and window lock before settling into bed. Maybe it's the unsettledness in our hearts as we watch our son drive away the first time after getting his license to operate a car. We look down one road – the road of fear – and we see lots of things we can say and do, and perhaps we even think it will help. The pull to run down that road, scurrying here and there, adjusting this or that, worrying about everything, is very strong. It has the power of habit. We've run that road so many times and it does offer some satisfying excitement: and a sense of accomplishing something, even though we have to admit it never lessens the fear that started the whole thing. The other road – the road of obedience – is filled with the promises of God that, after all, He is still in charge of His world and, more specifically, our lives. While not appearing to offer the chance to accomplish something, this road does offer rest and a better kind of safety. It also allows us to applaud God rather than wonder just what He's doing about all this.

At this point we stand at the decision point of belief, of demonstrated faith. We can choose to act in faith, or in unbelief. But wait a minute! Who are we really? Are we those who are blown here and there by every gust of news, by every display of brokenness this world offers up and by every story or piece of gossip that crosses the thresholds of our minds? Certainly part of who we are is susceptible to these things, but it's the part that longs to control beyond our opportunity or ability. But who we really are – daughters of the King, indwelt by His Spirit – recognizes the warning signs here. Living out our true, redeemed identity, we have become increasingly aware of God's greatness as we've studied His ways in history. We've seen His faithfulness proven over and over, and we've begun keeping a journal of the ways He has demonstrated Himself to our family time after time. Over time reliance on Him – nurtured through a deepening appreciation for His Word as it has been read and preached – has come to replace fearful action as our first response. Consequently, we've come to know what rest in times of trouble really feels like. We've come to understand with Paul (see Phil. 4:7) that 'peace, which surpasses all comprehension'. We are at peace, even though we can't understand why we should be on a human level. When we choose obedience, based on the truth of God that has permeated our souls, we find a rest, a peace, a comfort, and a courage to obey that overwhelms the temptations to fear and control that Satan puts in our paths.

As women our lives are very complex: the challenges to daily belief come in at so many moments, in so many packages. In the midst of it all, we simply must remember who we are and whose we are. As Christ-following women, our hearts are most at rest, most complete, most feminine according to God's definition, when they are focused on His gracious love and faithfulness to us. This isn't a new concept. When we trust Him and when we obey Him we find a sense of daily well-being that truly is better by far.

CHAPTER THIRTEEN

Epilogue: 'It's beyond me'

SEVERAL years ago, I took a long look at the ministry of preaching and pastoring that Christ had entrusted to me. It wasn't easy and it wasn't fun. Some of those who participated in the critique probably didn't realize that the darts they threw in anger were used by God in a good way. What I learned was that, for the most part, I had been producing 'water bottle' Christians. Here's what I mean.

In Southern California where I live almost everyone carries around a water bottle of some sort (more and more we are seeing re-useable models, because friends don't let friends drink out of plastic!). Our water bottles are portable fountains of refreshment. Every morning – and throughout the day – we fill them up with water and take sips and drinks to refresh ourselves while driving, working, walking, reading or whatever occupies our time. Simply put, we fill up the bottle for our own use. It's all about us, by us, and for us.

In too many ways I saw my ministry as producing Christ-followers who viewed the privileges of Christ the same way we saw the water in our bottles. To better understand, think of the life of a believer in Jesus as a water bottle. Let's say they've made a commitment to really be invested in the Word and prayer. They've also understood the great benefit of being under the preaching of the Word and they enjoy being part of a Bible Study. Maybe they are even interested in increasing their knowledge and practice of Christian disciplines, so they often can be found reading a good book on some theological topic or biblical theme.

In a way, all of these things can be like the refreshing water that fills up their bottle. They get up in the morning, read the Bible and some spiritual 'water' finds its way into their bottle; as they pray, they're filled up a bit more, and so on. During the day, when they feel a bit discouraged, they try to remember what they've read or how their time in prayer was or what that great author had to say in that book they've been reading. In a real way, they've come to see their life as in need of 'filling up' with the blessings of God so that, when needed, those same blessings can be useful in keeping them on track, refuelling their lives with joy and purpose, or even helping them to avoid temptation as they pursue the obedience option. Simply put, they've filled up with Christ for their own use. Like the real water bottle, their Christianity has become all about them, by them, and for them.

As their pastor, I began to realize that my efforts were helping to produce 'water bottle' Christians who were almost exclusively the end users of the blessings of God. Ouch! So I decided it was time for my perspective to be radically altered, to have my deformed outlook reformed according to God's Word. When I looked at the teachings of the apostles more closely, I found out that Christ never intended for His people – His church – to be the end users of all the wonderful promises, gifts and blessings that flow from His love.

Rather than be 'water bottle' Christians who fill up for personal benefit alone, He invites us to fill up with Christ for the purpose of righteous overflow in our world. It is through this overflow that His workmanship shines forth. This brings it all together, even as it changes everything.

Bringing it all together

In chapter three we learned that God didn't save us for us, but for Him. Since then, we've traced out the path of the obedience option and the privilege of growing an overwhelming kind of faith. Along the way, you may have slipped back into thinking that the blessings of faith and obedience were yours *for you!* But now we understand that the plan of God is so much bigger than that. He has rescued us for Himself so that, through lives transformed by the obedience option, His workmanship will be undeniable to everyone watching. But this doesn't happen on autopilot. As we've learned, the power of Christ in us is best recognized as our diligence for Christ is more and more realized. And what is the goal of it all? That our lives will overflow with the goodness and grace of Christian virtue, character, and obedience because through this overflow, God is authentically advertised as the supremely powerful and loving sovereign of the universe. The world is dying – literally – to know just that.

This changes everything

If you really understand all that is involved in the obedience option, then you'll also understand that it changes everything. Obeying Christ is always the best option, but it was never meant to bring us blessings to collect, save, hoard, and selfishly use. God's graces are never labelled 'for personal use only'. When we stop living around the edges of what it means to follow Christ, and dive into the middle of it, we'll find that the pursuit of Christ and all He is and gives takes on a much grander, much more noble, perspective. We'll begin to see our lives as funnels rather than canisters, as hoses rather than reservoirs, as water-falls rather than water bottles.

We'll begin to understand that, as we read the Bible, it isn't just for us any longer. It's actually for Bob at work, who is going through some tough family problems and is working up the nerve to ask some hard questions of us, since he heard we love Christ.

We'll come to see that our prayer time isn't just for us, but is also for those like Jim and Patty, across the street, who we keep ignoring because their lifestyle doesn't please us. Apparently, God needs to remind us of His grace toward outsiders and to re-align our hearts with His.

We'll come to recognize that sitting under the teaching of the Word or memorizing paragraphs from the Bible aren't just for our benefit but also for that guy at Starbucks who, after we engage him in conversations enough mornings, will feel free to ask us, 'How in the world can you think that the Bible is true?'

We'll also begin to grasp that true obedience to Christ isn't measured simply by our perseverance in righteousness, but also by the way righteousness and grace, love and truth, courage and compassion ooze out from us in ever-overflowing waves of authentic Christianity. The great benefit of this is that we will no longer be the focus of our diligence, the goal of our Gospel. Ultimately, the obedience option is better by far simply because it transforms our lives from self-centred to Christ-centred; from locked onto our own agenda, to delighting in His; from consumed with our wellbeing to pre-occupied with what our world will do with this man, Jesus.

May the Lord continue to use His Word in the lives of His people, calling them to trust Him completely as they pursue each day with the knowledge that what He has for them through obedience is – truly and eternally – better by far. *Soli Deo Gloria*.

How to ruin your life

SOMETIMES the best way to see the consequences of our sin is to take it out of the darkness and hold it up to the light. Many years ago I did just that with the Bathsheba event in the life of David. The story is found in 2 Samuel 11 but let me turn it upside down for you, by using it to show you just how you can go about ruining your life. If you really think that living in disobedience is the better choice then you may as well do it the way David did.

Of course what follows is entirely facetious; I am not really suggesting that you intentionally order your life toward ruin. What I am trying to do is show you the stark reality involved should you even think about letting yourself enjoy the pleasures of sin for a season. Remember, sin may advertise pleasure but its ends are the ways of death.

So with a bit of tongue-in-cheek, here's a great strategy for bringing ruin to your life. While the story of David applies particularly to men in the area of sexual temptation, you ladies can use the same strategy to plunge into ruin in the areas where temptation stalks you.

You might want to grab a Bible and read through the story in 2 Samuel 11 as we walk through these four steps on *How to ruin your life*.

Step 1: Convince yourself that living an undisciplined life poses no risk

That is what David did. At the time when the armies and kings of the land were out fighting wars, David stayed home and, apparently, spent lots of time in bed. His days were his own. There is no sense from the author here that David had any order to his days, to his spiritual progress, or to his life in general. In fact, just the opposite is suggested by the way the story unfolds. David wasn't where he should have been; he wasn't gainfully occupied; he wasn't keeping careful watch over his emotions and desires; he wasn't pursuing righteousness, love and faith with those who called upon God from a pure heart; and he certainly wasn't running away from opportunities. All this left him vulnerable and weak. He didn't realize it until it was too late. He had somehow convinced himself that living an undisciplined life posed no real risk. After all, he was the most powerful man in the realm and a man after God's own heart. God said so Himself.

It's at this point that we see an important truth: Spiritual position can lead to spiritual laziness. Like David, it is easy for us to think that, having got to a certain position or level in our race of faith, we can coast a bit. Maybe we even have enough spiritual fortitude to allow ourselves to taste the pleasures of sin. Maybe we no longer need to pursue righteousness. Maybe we've got a storehouse full and can take a break. And maybe that break extends for some time, and we become convinced that we're still doing just fine. We've convinced ourselves that living an undisciplined life really poses no risk. Great start! Now we're ready to take the next step in bringing ruin to our lives.

Step 2: Allow yourself to act according to your impulses rather than your commitments

David got out of bed one evening and took a stroll on his roof top. As the king, he probably had the highest roof and the best view. As he surveyed the city, he saw beautiful Bathsheba bathing on her rooftop. At that point, David stood looking down two roads. His impulse pointed him down the road of lust, adultery and spiritual death. His commitments would have called him down the road of obedience. They would have, except for the fact that his lack of spiritual discipline had allowed those commitments to God and righteousness to become dull and weak. You know the story. In David's mind there was no wrestling, no struggle to maintain the purity of his heart or of his marital relationship. He simply let his sexual impulse lead the way.

One of the great side benefits of an undisciplined life is the fact that it can round off the edges of our commitments. After all, we certainly don't want to be one of those religious fanatics! Maybe our rigidity in the pursuit of righteousness isn't all that good for us, and so we back away from our disciplined strategy of obedience. As we do so, we find that the impulses we've worked so hard to keep in check rise to the surface. Of course, we know they're there and we're vigilant. But over time, they become stronger and more comfortable. We even feed them a bit and find that it feels good. Then it happens. We're doing something when suddenly a sinful impulse barges its way into our mind. In the past it would have been held in check by the cage of our faith, but apparently we left the cage-door open and we're in trouble. Giving in to the impulse is so much easier than it should be and we're blind to any negative consequences. Maybe acting according to impulse rather than commitment isn't all that bad. After all, it feels so good. Now we're really on our way to ruin.

Step 3: When your sin is about to be found out, pour all your energy into cover-up rather than confession

After David had slept with Bathsheba she became pregnant. Now David faced a crisis. His sin would be made public unless he took steps to cover it up. The author makes no mention of whether or not David even considered coming clean before God and his people. What we do see is that David threw all his efforts into an elaborate plan to hide his sin. You can read the story yourself, and you'll see that in all of the plans, Bathsheba's husband Uriah is the one with integrity, with true commitment to God. God's king has no integrity, while the Hittite soldier has plenty. This is most seen in the final part of David's plan which is carefully detailed in a letter written to the commanding general of the army. The plan called for the army to desert Uriah, leaving him defenceless in the face of the enemy. Ironically, David asked Uriah to carry the letter. The plan depended on Uriah's integrity not to open the envelope carrying his own death sentence. Uriah maintained his integrity and it cost him his life.

When the gorilla gets out of the cage, chaos and tragedy always result. At first the damage may be small, almost inconsequential. But, eventually, it will be noticeable, people will start to wonder and we'll have to decide on a course of action: Will we confess or cover-up? If you really want to ruin your life, you've got to cover up your sin. You've simply got to deal with the mess and not the gorilla. After all, it's really not that big a mess. You can get it cleaned up if you work really hard, lie quite a bit and count on the trust you've built in your relationships over time. You're a good person and folks will understand. That's so much easier than strengthening the cage and re-capturing the gorilla.

Step 4: Convince yourself you got away with it – so you can do it all again

At the end of 2 Samuel 11 David's cover-up appears to have worked. Uriah is dead. Bathsheba becomes his wife, and a child is born. No one seems to notice; no one seems to care, least of all

David. It looks like he got away with all of it. No harm done. I am sure David was relieved. He may have even secretly determined not to do that again. Whatever the case, David believes it's over; he cleaned up the mess and got away with it.

The key to ruining your life is building up a false confidence that the sinful ways you've chosen really haven't hurt you. You've lived under God's radar. You've come to believe that, unless something terrible happens to you, your sin has no consequence. All this allows you to relax even more, feed your impulses, get better and better at cover-up and deceit, and repeat the cycle time after time. As you do this, your ruin will become more and more apparent until ultimately you are left with no good choices and a life full of regret.

You'll notice that at the end of 2 Samuel 11:27 God enters the story again. Up to this point it did look like David was operating behind God's back, beyond His notice. But that wasn't the case. In one devastating sentence, God is back. And His position is made clear: 'But the thing that David had done was evil in the sight of the LORD.'

Always remember that the consequences of sin are real, and deep. They may masquerade as inconsequential, but God sees and recognizes evil as evil, and will deal with it. When we walk the path of disobedience, we are preferring evil and rejecting good. In this way, we are rejecting God; we are not walking in faith. Our gracious and loving heavenly Father will use discipline to bring us back into line and often the first step in that discipline is to let the consequences of our sin fall on us. Just ask David.

When all is said and done ...

The truth is simple: we can't thumb our noses at God and escape the consequences. That's why it only makes sense to see obedience as our very best option. As we pursue righteousness, faith, love, and peace with those who call upon God from pure hearts, we will come more and more to see the truth: Faith is a life-dominating conviction that all God has for me through obedience is better by far than anything the world or Satan can offer through selfishness and sin.

How to gain your life

THROUGHOUT this book I have made some assumptions. First among them was that you – my reader – started from a position of prizing God and His ways. More than that I hoped you understood the connection between loving God and delighting in holy living, in obeying what God says is best and right. Finally I believed as I wrote that the material in this book could help you in pursuing that obedience, that it could enlighten you and encourage you to view the rewards of righteousness as truly better by far. If that has occurred then God be praised.

But I also realized that reading this book might have opened your eyes to another, more disturbing possibility. Maybe somewhere along the line you had to admit that you really do not think righteousness is all it's advertised to be. Maybe you even came to the place where you were honest enough with yourself to admit that you don't prize holy living and that you're not really sure God always has it right. Perhaps this realization caused you to stop and consider just what a lack of desire for righteous living says about you, about your soul's connection with God. Are you justified in calling yourself a Christ-follower? Or are you really just following the crowd that is following Him? These are very important questions, too important to ignore because they speak to the gravest issues in this world as well as in the next.

So let's have a go at the core truth that is at stake in life. Let's listen to the message God has been declaring from the beginning of time, and see how it affects your life and just what your options are.

In the beginning God ...

That's where everything has to start. God has always existed and everything that exists somehow has come into being because of Him. The Bible confirms this and declares that God is not only the creator of all things but that He created all things for a specific purpose: to display His greatness and His glory. Creation was to be God's masterpiece – and it was until sin came in bringing death and its own brand of pollution and corruption. Like an invisible toxin, sin came into God's handcrafted system and immediately began reproducing itself. In came death, with all of its horrors. In came brokenness, in its myriad examples. The devastating effects of sin became evident over time as brother murdered brother and both creation and society spiralled downward into physical and spiritual corruption of the gravest kind. That spiral has continued unabated to our day and all we need to do is read a newspaper for confirmation. What God made good, sin made bad.

God certainly would have had good reasons to turn His back on humanity in the wake of Adam's blatant disobedience. He could have justly left us all to the consequences of our sinful ways. He could have watched as we all lived the way we wanted to live, willingly and joyfully choosing the road of independence from Him. But God's amazing love for His creation prevailed and, instead, He initiated the most dramatic rescue and reclamation operation ever conceived. He decided to demonstrate His glory by being gracious and merciful to those who neither deserved it nor could do anything to merit His loving attention.

Throughout the Old Testament of the Bible God's promise to fix all that sin had broken was told through the adventures of the nation of Israel. God decided to preview His plan to reclaim creation through them. In the laws He gave them, as well as in the religious rituals He commanded of them, God carefully brought His plan to light. Their sin left them in a precarious position. It made them guilty before God. But God's forgiveness was extended to them graciously, through faith alone, on the basis of His promise to one day send the One who would turn curse into blessing. Their obedience of faith that God was trustworthy, and would keep that promise was shown in the way they lived and in the sacrifices they brought to Him. Year after year those sacrifices were understood as previews of the one great sacrifice that God Himself would someday make to deal with the problem of sin and guilt once and for all. Those Israelites who walked by faith understood this and looked forward with great hope to that day.

Into the world came God the Son ...

After thousands of years God's promise was finally fulfilled. One day in Jerusalem John saw Jesus walking and cried out, 'Behold, the Lamb of God who takes away the sin of the world!' (John 1:29). Here, finally, was the promised one. For centuries, as the Israelites sacrificed lambs at Passover, they knew that one day God's Lamb would come to fulfill what the sacrificial system only previewed. And it had finally happened!

But Jesus would have to prove that He was the Saviour. Many had come before claiming to be the promised one, the Jewish Messiah. Each one had been compared to the list of things the Old Testament prophets declared Messiah would do and been found lacking. That list included things like opening blind eyes and deaf ears, healing the lame and the leper, and even making the dead to live again. These were not things that anyone could accomplish unless they were truly God.

Through the writings of Matthew, Mark, Luke, and John we can critique Jesus ourselves. Like the people of His day we can watch as He opens the eyes of the blind, cleanses the lepers, heals hundreds of sick people and even raises the dead. We can hear Him say something that can change our lives forever, 'Your sins are forgiven.'

This amazing story and its significance for you is wrapped up in two simple verses found in the New Testament:

> For God so loved the world, that He gave His only begotten Son, that whoever believes in Him shall not perish, but have eternal life. (John 3:16)

> ... giving thanks to the Father, who has qualified us to share in the inheritance of the saints in Light. For He rescued us from the domain of darkness, and transferred us to the kingdom of His beloved Son, in whom we have redemption, the forgiveness of sins. (Col. 1:12-14)

God the Son took our sin ...

There is a great mystery in all this. If you're really thinking well you recognize that simply agreeing with the Bible about Jesus doesn't really change the fact that you and I still have a sin problem. How can a just God forgive you and me when we deserve the penalty the law of God has set for those who break it? Does God just let us get away with it if we promise to be good from now on? How is that just?

The answer is amazing and yet so simple. Here's how it works. Remember that God made all things to display His glory but sin ruined it all. On top of that, sin placed God in the position of having to be the righteous Judge, handing out the just penalties we deserve. But also remember that God's love moved Him to bring a resolution to the sin problem that allowed sinners to escape the penalty of their sin. At this point God's love was seemingly at odds with His justice. He had to punish sin in order to be just. Yet He longed to forgive sinners out of His great love. Something incredible had to happen to allow both His justice and His love to proceed unfettered.

That something was the work of God the Son, Jesus Christ. When Jesus came to earth He really had a two-fold mission. First He needed to demonstrate that He was the promised one, God in the flesh, sent to redeem creation from the brokenness of sin. Then He had to do the work necessary for that redemption to be accomplished. Here's how He did it, as explained by the apostle Paul in 2 Corinthians 5:21: 'He [God the Father] made Him who knew no sin [God the Son] to be sin on our behalf, so that we might become the righteousness of God in Him.'

God the Father is also the Judge of all things. God the Son willingly died as our substitute, taking on Himself our sin and our guilt. Then He withstood the full, unobstructed wrath of the court of heaven for sin. He took our punishment as our substitute. And He did it willingly, joyfully and out of great love.

But if you're tracking with me you realize that our sin was really only half the problem. Even if God figured a way to take our sin and guilt out of the way we still were left with the awful reality that we were broken, corrupted by the toxins of sin. We had a bad record but we also had a bad heart. Pretty bad situation.

Amazingly, God was up to the challenge. He took care of our bad record as God the Son paid the debt we owed. Then He took care of our bad heart by crediting the righteousness of Jesus Christ to our account. That's what Paul means in the verse above (2 Cor. 5:21).

He made Him who knew no sin to be sin on our behalf → He took our sin and paid our debt
that we might become the righteousness of God in Him → He gave us His righteousness

---

There it is, the great exchange, the amazing transaction, the deal of the century. We traded our sin for His righteousness, our guilt for His forgiveness, our brokenness for full acceptance into the family of God.

Now that's really good news, but there's even more: this is all ours for free. The forgiveness God offers us because of Jesus' life, death, and resurrection can be ours at no cost. It's free; but it's not cheap. It's free to us; but it cost God the Son His life. What He accomplished for us is extended to us and experienced by us as we come to believe that God is telling the truth. We believe God's statements about Jesus and sin and forgiveness, and entrust our eternal well-being to God on the basis of that truth. We turn from our sinful ways and selfish agenda to follow Jesus Christ in obedience. We find that God's forgiveness and a new life are ours, and that living for His glory is our very best option. It's not a trick and it isn't a scam. It's just life as our Creator meant it to be lived, and you can have it. You can gain your life. When you do you'll find that all God has for you as a Christ-follower if better by far than anything this world can dangle before your eyes. He'll show you why living for His glory beats trying to manufacture your own, and how satisfying it is to partner with Him in changing the world. And it's all free.